High Performance Racing

High Performance Racing

John Merricks
&
Ian Walker

fernhurst
B O O K S

First published 1996 by Fernhurst Books,
Duke's Path, High Street, Arundel, West Sussex,
BN18 9AJ, UK. Tel: 01903 882277.

Printed and bound in Great Britain

British Library Cataloguing in Publication Data.
A catalogue record for this book is available
from the British Library.

ISBN 1 898660 30 1

Photographs
The authors and publisher would like to thank
the following for their photographic assistance.
The Laser Centre for the loan of a Laser 5000
and Anna Cooper for the loan of the Laser 4000 .
Shots of these boats were taken by Chris Davies
at Hayling Island Sailing Club from Frank
Dunster's RIB. Thanks to the club for their
hospitality. Other photos supplied by Premiere
on behalf of Mars, sponsor to Merricks &
Walker, and by Peter Bentley. Photos of the 49er
courtesy of LDC Racing Sailboats.

Edited by Tim Davison

Cover design by Simon Balley

DTP by Creative Byte, Poole

Printed and bound by
Hillman Printers, Frome

Contents

Part 3   Technique & Boatspeed

Part 4   The Racing

Part 5   Planning to Succeed

INTRODUCTION

The 1990s has been a period of rapid change in both the form and the format of small boat racing.

One key change is the development of new light, fast, exciting designs, most of which sport fully-battened mainsails and asymmetric spinnakers flown from a fixed or retracting bowsprit. These ideas stem from the remarkable success of the International 14 when it switched to twin trapezes and masthead asymmetric spinnakers. The developments were made increasingly viable by the advent of new stronger and lighter construction methods using carbon fibre and foam sandwich, and by Mylar sails.

Part one shows how to get started in a new class with a high-tec rig. We look at the theory behind different rigs and show how to prepare your rig, boat, body and mind to compete with the best.

Part two will serve as your manual to master the new boathandling techniques

of these skiff-type dinghies and small keelboats.

Part three teaches you how to go fast and really get the best out of your boat. We concentrate on both upwind and downwind legs and consider techniques and sail shapes for all wind conditions.

The other big change on the racing scene is the shift towards much shorter courses and smaller fleets. This has come about largely as a result of the ISF's decision that the Olympic classes will no longer race solely around the old 'Olympic course' (more commonly known as the triangle, sausage, triangle) which featured long legs and usually just one long race per day. Races are now shorter and we have a lot more of them. We also have different course layouts, the most common being the Olympic trapezoid and Super Cup (windward-leeward) courses which often feature gates instead of rounding marks.

Part four is devoted to this new style of racing and in it we look at each course layout and its relevant features, together with the changes in strategy that these courses demand.

Since starting our Olympic 470 campaign in 1993 for the 1996 Atlanta Olympic Games we have been faced with many hard decisions in planning for success. We have not only learned from our successes and failures but have watched many other campaigns succeed or fail.

Part five highlights our own sailing philosophy and shows how we plan our campaigns. We look at the many areas that need to be considered when 'planning to succeed' and we will help you not only set yourself realistic goals in sailing, but fulfill them.

Who is this book for?

We hope this book will not only appeal to those racing the 'new' classes or competing around the 'new' courses but also to anyone who wants to improve their results in the more traditional high-performance dinghy and keelboat classes.

Sailing, and in particular trying to get around race courses faster than anyone else, has given us both great pleasure and we hope there is something in this book to help everyone enjoy and improve their racing. We hope you enjoy reading it - and good luck out on the water!

John Merricks
Ian Walker

On top of the world. Merricks and Walker in action.

PART ONE
PREPARATION

1 PREPARATION

PREPARING THE BOAT

Many high-performance dinghies and keelboats are strict one-designs and leave little opportunity for improving the layout of fittings and systems in the boat. Even in these classes, however, there will always be boats that are better prepared than many in the fleet. The key areas that are generally easy to address and yet can make a considerable difference to performance are: weight; simplicity; centralising the boom; eliminating friction; reliability; legality; hull surface; slot gaskets and foils.

Weight

The leading sailors have always gone to great lengths to optimise weight. Key weight-saving ideas are outlined below.

1. The major influence on weight is water and if your boat lives outside it is well worth investing in a reliable watertight cover. It is also a good idea to dry out the boat periodically in a garage with a heater (or preferably a de-humidifier) and is a must before any big event.

2. Eliminate all leaks into the tanks (remember 1 litre of water = 1 kg). Fittings are the major offenders and these should all be sealed with silicone sealant. In boats with a daggerboard take care not to damage the back of the case by running aground, which can also cause leaking. Screw in the hatch covers properly using good rubber seals and a splattering of either silicone or Vaseline – taking particular care if your boat is self-draining. Check your tanks are watertight by blowing gently (too hard may cause damage) into them through a bung hole. If pressure is lost find the leaks by spreading soapy water over potentially dodgy areas (fittings, cracks, joins etc.).

3. Reduce water retained in ropes by using the thinnest possible control lines made out of modern materials that soak up less weight (Spectra, Dyneema etc.). Taper ropes to leave only the outer core except where you pull them or where they cleat.

4. Use the smallest and lightest fittings for any given job but don't sacrifice performance (e.g. low friction) for weight.

5. Any weight saved in the ends of the boat or in the rig is particularly worthwhile as this will improve the pitching moment of the boat.

This spinnaker sheet is tapered from 6 mm where the crew holds it to 4 mm and then 3 mm for the last part to the sail.

The KISS principle (Keep It Simple Stupid)

Keep the boat as simple and tidy as possible. You must be able to adjust the key rig controls easily (and from the trapeze if necessary), but over-complicating systems normally leads either to gear failure or more chances of foul ups at key moments. Use simple elastic takeaways on the tails of ropes to keep the boat tidy and prevent tangling of loose ends – provided the takeaways themselves do not start getting in the way. The kicking strap and cunningham are the key controls as you should be adjusting them regularly, so they must have plenty of purchase and be to hand whether you're hiking or trapezing.

Using a loop system (right) to attach the trapeze elastic to the rings may be fast to rig, but can lead to re-hooking accidentally to the elastic loop in a tack or gybe.

Note how in this Laser 5000 the end of the mainsheet is attached to the vang (kicking strap) and the cunningham is attached to the jibsheets so both can be adjusted from the wire.

Centralising the boom

Keeping the boom as near the centreline as possible has a noticeable effect on pointing ability and overall upwind performance. If you have a mainsheet hoop there is little you can do to help this, but if you have mainsheet strops you can adjust them to keep the system as close to block-to-block as possible for any given rake. If the class rules allow, it is well worth having a system which pulls the blocks to windward slightly so you can get the boom bang on the centreline. Always try to make the system self-releasing in the tacks so your tacking is not affected.

Eliminating friction

Friction in systems occurs for several reasons:

1. The lead is wrong so the rope is rubbing on something.

2. The rope is too thick.

3. The blocks are too small or are worn out (they don't last forever).

Eliminating friction will make adjustments easier and help the ropes last longer, reducing the amount of boatwork needed.

Particular attention must be paid to the spinnaker halyard. In their 1993 campaign for the International 14 Worlds Ian and his crew Chris Fox could never understand why James Hartley and Ian Tillett were so much faster at spinnaker hoists and drops until they drew their boat for the Super Cup final. Lying in second place behind Tim Robinson and Bruce Grant they were able to drop their spinnaker more efficiently and pass them at the leeward mark before going on to win the race. Tim and Bruce were clearly struggling and we now knew why – they had drawn Ian and Chris' boat with its high friction halyard for the final! A better angle of lead, a thinner halyard and two new blocks was all it took to reduce the friction in Ian's halyard.

Check that the mainsheet strops are identical in length.

With the mainsheet strops too short the boom is way off the centreline unless you oversheet the leech of the main.

Mainsheet strops the correct length for this rake. The boom is nearer the centreline with the correct leech tension.

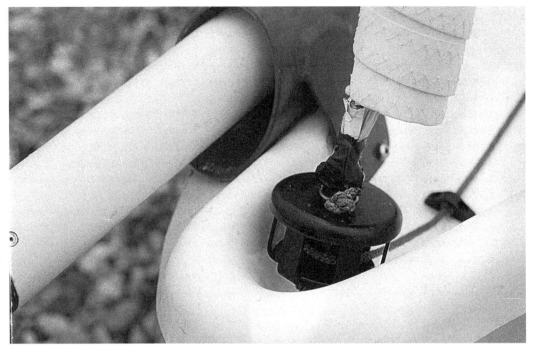

It is particularly important to tape up fittings on the bow as the spinnaker can easily catch and rip. This is especially true in boats with a spinnaker chute.

Reliability

Gear failure is one of the most common dinghy park excuses for not doing well, but most of it is avoidable. Here are a few tips to prevent unnecessary breakages.

1. Tape up all sharp edges and clevis pins to reduce the likelihood of the pins coming out or a sail getting ripped.

2. Replace ropes if they look worn. Try to save money by 'end for ending' ropes from time to time to move the points of wear.

3. Regularly check key fittings such as shackles, rudder pintles, slot gaskets, spreader brackets, trapeze harness hooks and toestraps, particularly after windy races.

4. Think about disaster scenarios and how you would fix them during a race. Always carry a length of spare rope (preferably with a hook on one end to save time tying a knot) in case something does break.

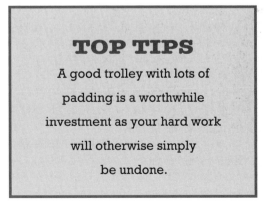

TOP TIPS

A good trolley with lots of padding is a worthwhile investment as your hard work will otherwise simply be undone.

At Hyeres Olympic Regatta in 1995 we sailed a race in winds gusting over 35 knots. After the race we checked the boat over and spotted a kink in the back of the mast track. On close inspection we found the spreader bracket had compressed into the back of the mast. We put in our spare mast for the next day and sailed two more races in up to 30 knots of wind. Winning both races and the series, we reflected on the fact that the other mast would certainly have broken and taken with it our hopes of winning overall.

During the 1993 Kiel week regatta in the 420 class John & crewman Ian Lovering were in the lead in survival conditions. Just before lowering the spinnaker at the leeward mark in preparation for the last beat the team realized that the port trapeze wire had come unhooked from the terminal on the mast. The problem was solved by quickly dropping the spinnaker, tying the spinnaker halyard to the top of the

trapeze wire, then rehoisting the halyard to hold their lead.

Legality

Most classes have strict rules and you must stick to them. 'Dodgy' gains are never worth the worry and hassle they cause at regattas. Always turn up at an event confident that your boat and sails are legal. In classes like the Laser 4000 and Laser 5000 always make sure you have the racks out as far as you can and are carrying the least lead possible while still being just within the rules.

Outer hull surface

At our target regattas we pay special attention to the outer hull surface. There are many differences of opinion on how laminar the flow

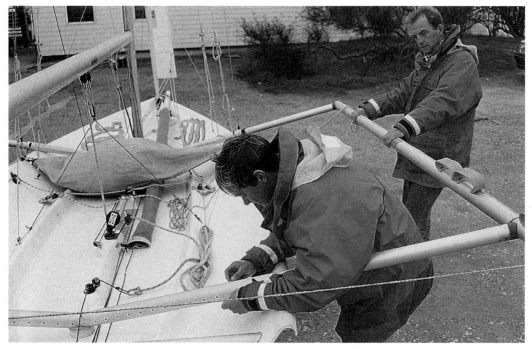

In weight-equalisation boats set the racks precisely before racing.

Glued Mylar strips provide little turbulence, but are hard to maintain.

Fair off the bailer until it's like silk.

is around a dinghy hull and how important it is to have a perfect finish. Some people swear by a matt finish and some will try their utmost to have a highly polished finish. We try our best to achieve the following with our outer hull.

1. Fairness. We fill scratches, chips and hollows, and fair-in the bailers and slot gaskets.

2. Polished finish. We use very high grade (1200) wet-and-dry and a polish.

3. Cleanliness. When launching from a harbour with oily deposits we take particular care to hose down and clean the outer hull and foils with washing up liquid or Jif. One of the main arguments against a matt finish is that it is more susceptible to picking up and retaining dirt than a gloss/polished finish.

In the 1995 PACT Americas Cup campaign the hull finish was maintained by a rota of sailors who would take their turn to fair and polish parts of the hull instead of physical training in the morning. This rota included the skipper and helmsman and also helped to serve as a team-building exercise.

4. Slot gaskets. We are convinced that these are a major source of drag and recommend glued Mylar strips (available from most

sailmakers). There is a danger that they can fall off, but this has never happened to us and we use two-part Evostick glue. Before gluing, roughen up both the hull and the Mylar strips and thoroughly clean and dry them (using Acetone). They need replacing regularly and careful treatment to prevent creasing. They are not recommended if you have little time for boatwork or have poor launching/recovery facilities at your club.

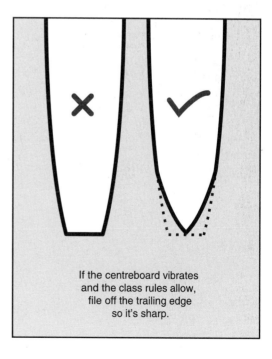

If the centreboard vibrates and the class rules allow, file off the trailing edge so it's sharp.

Notice how much this 49er mast (and in particular the fibreglass topmast) bends, even without sailing loads.

Foils

Many high performance boats have one-design foils and there is no freedom of choice within the rules. In these classes the main improvements that can be made are in surface finish. Treat the foils in the same way as the outer hull surface but give them more care as they take more punishment. It is well worth investing in good foil bags, and taking care of your foils when ashore.

Vibration

In some boats there is a humming sensation when sailing, particularly at high speeds, and this can often be cured by improving the centreboard case packing/lining or sharpening the trailing edge of the centreboard (within the class rules).

Open classes

In classes where there is an element of choice in foil or keel design we would recommend that you start with the class norm before trying anything different. Nine times out of ten the class norm will be good enough, as that is how it got so popular in the first place!

PREPARING THE RIG

The Mast

While many factors combine to dictate the racing performance of a sailboat, few are as important as the mast/mainsail combination. Many top sailors are obsessed with finding the best section available.

As people analysed the superb performance of Peter Blake's Team New Zealand in winning the 1995 America's Cup, the biggest difference between them and their opposition appears to have been the section and characteristics of their mast and the effect that had on main-sail shapes.

Most of the emerging new classes allow only one section, while many high performance classes have strict limitations on the mast section and rigging. A few development classes still permit radical ideas and exotic materials, and act as a testing ground.

Aluminium. This is still the leading mast material on the grounds of cost and reliability of performance. Most sailors are familiar , with how aluminium masts react and the abundance of different sections and tapers provide sailors with most of the characteristics they may require.

Carbon. For any given stiffness carbon masts offer considerable weight saving over aluminium because carbon is stronger and can withstand greater compressive loads. Weight is also saved by not having to have a uniform section. More material can be added to specific parts of the mast to withstand local loads. Similarly the mast can be sanded in specific areas to 'soften' it at that point. The downsides to carbon are currently the extra cost, its brittleness and the lack of understanding of exactly how far the masts can be pushed compared with aluminium.

Fibreglass top-section. It is a growing trend on the new 'skiff type' boats to have an aluminium section as far as the hounds and then a fibreglass tip, which is often supported by upper shrouds. The idea is that as a boat becomes overpowered the topmast will bend backwards and slightly to leeward to de-power the top of the sail. This 'gust response' makes the boat easier to sail because less mainsheet is eased so the jib slot stays open and drive is retained in the base of the main. The key is the stiffness and elasticity of the topmast which re-powers the mainsail in the lulls by straightening and tightening the leech.

It is crucial that the tip is the right stiffness and that the upper shrouds are set correctly. It is also very important that the luff curve in the head of the mainsail fits the range of bend of the mast tip.

Weight

Wherever possible you should try to keep the weight of the mast and rigging to a minimum. Stripping the outer core off Spectra running rigging is one easy way of saving some weight.

Windage

The drag caused by windage is clearly demonstrated when you try to take down a mast on your own on a windy day. Always keep windage to a minimum. All the small things add up, so use thin jib and spinnaker halyards, take off the burgee and fixing, take the protest flags off the trapeze wires, or at least make all these things neater and more streamlined.

Standing rigging

The rigging of a mast is another highly complex subject which in itself could fill a book (see the Fernhurst title *Sailpower*).

Here is an outline of how the rigs of most popular high performance classes operate.

1. A single spreader rig as used on most boats without a masthead spinnaker.

Spreader angle. This is the main controlling influence over fore-and-aft mast bend. Swinging the spreaders back will bend the mast more and vice-versa. If the mast is not set up with enough pre-bend it will have a tendency to invert downwind under spinnaker.

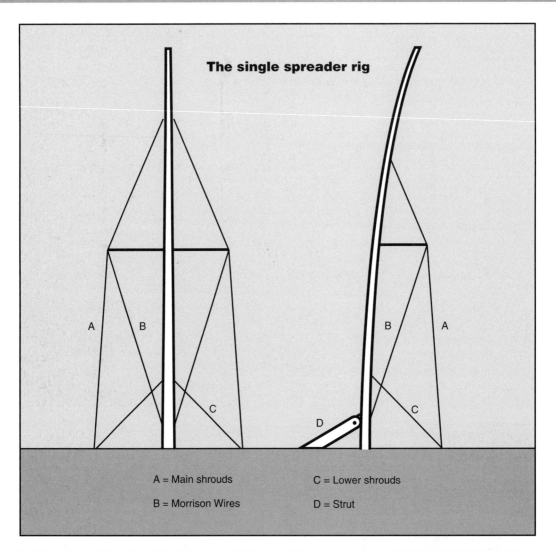

The single spreader rig

A = Main shrouds

B = Morrison Wires

C = Lower shrouds

D = Strut

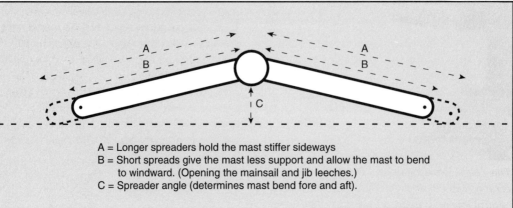

A = Longer spreaders hold the mast stiffer sideways
B = Short spreads give the mast less support and allow the mast to bend
    to windward. (Opening the mainsail and jib leeches.)
C = Spreader angle (determines mast bend fore and aft).

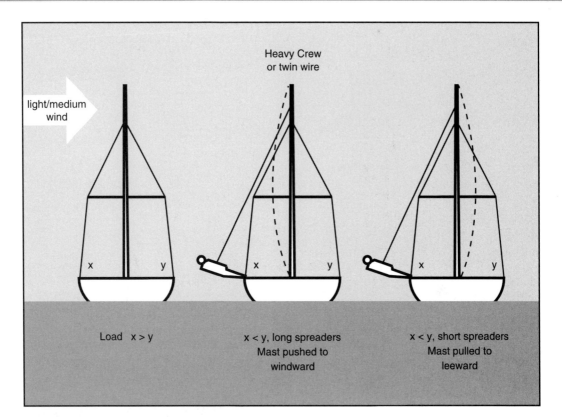

light/medium wind

Heavy Crew or twin wire

Load   x > y

x < y, long spreaders
Mast pushed to
windward

x < y, short spreaders
Mast pulled to
leeward

The 470 uses this wire-and-ferrule arrangement in place of mast chocks to control low mast bend precisely.

Spreader length. This controls the sideways bend of the mast. Shorter spreaders allow the mast to bend to windward in the middle, depowering the mainsail and opening the mainsail leech and the jib slot. Long spreaders have the opposite effect, holding the mast in column and powering up the rig. Note that in trapeze boats with a big crew or twin-wire boats in light/medium winds the weight on the trapeze is greater than the wind strength load on the weather shroud so the leeward shroud finishes up tighter than the windward one. The mast will be 'pulled' to leeward if short spreaders are fitted whereas long spreaders will push the middle of the mast to windward. This is opposite to what you might normally expect!

Tuning a two-spreader rig.

Shrouds. In conjunction with the jib halyard, these dictate the rake and rig tension.

Jib halyard. Adjusts the rig tension and therefore both the jib luff sag and the rake as well.

Morrison wires. These force prebend (fore/aft bend) into the mast when tightened and are also essential to stop the mast inverting downwind on large dinghies like the Laser 5000. When tight they also support the mast sideways.

Lower shrouds. These straighten the mast low down when tightened, and also support the mast sideways. They take much of the load imposed by the vang or gnav.

Strut. Controls fore/aft bend low down. (Preferred by some in the International 14 as it

doesn't hold the mast stiff sideways like lowers, therefore allowing some sideways bend in windy weather.) The strut is an especially powerful tool for prebending the mast in light winds or depowering the mainsail on a tight reach.

Ram/chocks. Most common in boats with a foredeck or spaceframe, these also dictate the fore/aft bend low down.

2. Two-spreader rig as used in most twin-trapeze dinghies with a masthead spinnaker.

Spreader angle/length. These operate in a similar way to a single spreader rig except they are only one part of a more complex rig and therefore have a smaller individual effect.

Shrouds/jib halyard. These also operate as on a

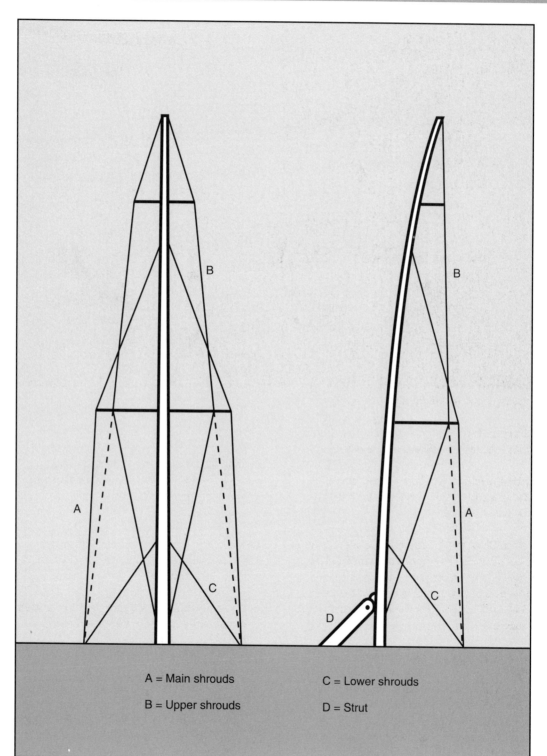

A = Main shrouds   C = Lower shrouds

B = Upper shrouds   D = Strut

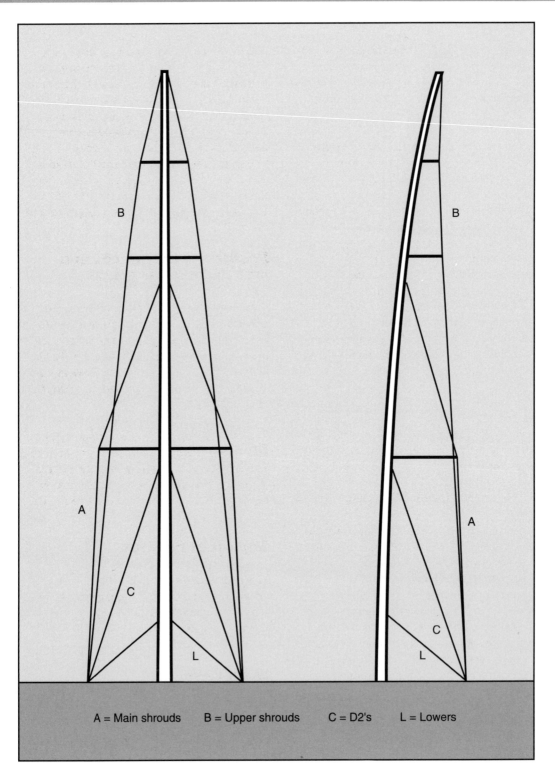

A = Main shrouds   B = Upper shrouds   C = D2's   L = Lowers

one-spreader rig. Care must be taken to keep on enough rig tension in windy weather on a twin trapeze boat because if the windward shroud goes very slack the mast can fail to windward.

Upper shrouds. An upper shroud can either be independent of the lower spreader or be attached at the end or middle of the spreader, before leading down and being attached to either the chainplate or mast base. Tightening the upper shrouds will always bend the topmast back, and support it sideways. If they pass through the lower spreader, and particularly if they then attach to the mast base, tightening the uppers will push pre-bend into the whole mast and hold it straighter/support it sideways. Note that sideways mast bend can be effective when overpowered as it depowers the mainsail and opens the jib slot.

Ram/chocks, strut, and lowers all operate as on the one-spreader rig, but their effect is very much restricted to lower mast bend. Be careful not to invert the mast low down by having too many chocks on.

3. Three-spreader 18 ft skiff rig

Essentially the same as the two-spreader rig, except there are two sets of upper spreaders, both because of the mast size and the high load of such a large masthead spinnaker. This rig has excellent gust response due to its fibreglass tip and because the lower spreaders are independent of the upper shrouds. A skiff mast can be reduced in size for windy weather by lowering it in its 'stump' and shortening the upper and lower shrouds and jib luff.

4. Single-spreader keelboat rig

Essentially the same as the single-spreader

dinghy rig, but the masts are far stronger and stiffer. Less pre-bend is required to prevent inversion under spinnaker because the load is taken directly by the backstay which is also used to bend the mast, especially when the boat is overpowered. Mast bend is also controlled by the lowers, which when tightened straighten the mast both fore-and-aft and sideways. Forestay length is used to set the mast rake, while the shrouds are used to control the headsail luff sag and simply to hold the mast up.

Position of the hounds and trapeze take-off points

If you have a big crew or two trapezes, the position of the hounds and trapeze take-off points will also affect the bend of the mast as the crew exert a considerable load. In the International 14 we lowered ours to below the forestay take-off point to try and straighten the mast slightly.

The best example of this in action is in a 505 where 1995 World Champions Jeremy Robinson and Bill Masterman had a system to adjust the trapeze take-off point so that it would help to either power up or depower the mast/mainsail.

Mast foot position

This affects the balance of the boat and is a crucial starting point. We recommend that you start by copying the class average or the champion in your class.

Mast rake

All high-performance classes rake the mast back as the wind increases to maintain optimum upwind VMG. Increasing the rake has many effects, but these are the main three.

This boat is well set up, with the correct power for the conditions. Note that the helmsman has coiled the tail of the mainsheet, and keeps it in his tiller hand.

1. It moves the centre of effort of the rig back.

2. It forces more pre-bend into the mast for any given spreader setting (which depowers the rig).

3. It opens the jib slot (again, depowering the rig).

At the 1988 UK Youth championships , John & Ian were competing against each other in 420s . Racing in 18 knots & big waves on the second beat of the first race, the two boats were in the lead and neck-and-neck. That was until John's jib halyard sheave box exploded, which lengthened the jib luff and raked the mast aft several inches. After the breakage John's upwind speed was significantly better than before and he went on to win the race. The importance of rake was learned!

How much rake should I use?

Every class has a range of rakes to suit specific conditions. Once you have the rake settings calibrated it is best to set up the mast rake before the start according to the feel of the boat. If the mast is raked too far back the boat will feel underpowered and you will struggle to point. If the mast is too upright the boat will feel overpowered and will tend to stagger, especially in the gusts. In gusty conditions we recommend setting your rig up to work best in the lulls as you can always depower in the gusts using the cunningham. One good reason for doing this is that out of the start line, when you most need your speed, there tends to be less wind due to all the boats slowing the local windspeed.

Twin-Trapeze boats

It is absolutely crucial to have the rig set up for the correct amount of power as it is very hard to sail a boat that is continually either overpowered or underpowered.

For their 1993 International 14 World's Campaign (over the old long courses) Ian and Chris set up their boat so they could adjust the shrouds, jib halyard, uppers, cunningham and vang from the trapeze to ensure the right amount of power was retained in the rig. For short course racing they fixed the shrouds and jib halyard and relied on the cunningham/vang.

Keeping the mast in the boat

In most of the new high-performance classes there is considerable load on the mast because of the power being generated by high righting moments and large sailplans. It is very much part of racing to 'keep the mast in the boat' on windy days and this ability to compromise takes considerable judgement. Let's look at the most common forms of failure and how to avoid them.

Problem 1. Mast inversion downwind
This is caused by the forward pull of the spinnaker trying to turn the mast inside-out. Inversion typically happens when the boat nose-dives, thus slowing and loading up the rig.

Solutions

a. Set up the mast with more pre-bend if inversion looks likely (bolt swinging spreaders).

b. Pull hard on the cunningham to bend the mast backwards and depower the mainsail.

c. Do not over-ease the vang despite its

> # TOP TIPS
>
> 1. The mast/mainsail combination is extremely important for good boatspeed.
>
> 2. Choose a mast primarily because of its bend characteristics not just its weight.
>
> 3. Start off with standard class gear and settings before experimenting.
>
> 4. Wherever possible reduce weight and windage in the rigging.

depowering effect, because the mainsail leech holds the mast back.

d.   Sit back and don't nosedive.

e. Back off by sailing lower or easing the spinnaker just prior to planting the bow into the wave ahead.

Problem 2. Mast folding to windward upwind
Common in twin-trapeze boats when the windward shroud goes slack, particularly in waves.

Solutions

a. Pull on more rig tension (windward shroud should never go slack) and uppers if they

Our vang (kicking strap) gear spreads the load nicely and will help prevent boom failure.

pass through the lower spreader (this may be slower, so it's a compromise).

b. Lengthen the lower spreaders to give more sideways support.

c. Use a stiffer mast section (again this might be slower).

Problem 3. Mast folding to leeward

A direct result of broken or inadequate rigging, most common when nosediving.

Solutions

a. Stronger shrouds.

b. Check rigging and replace regularly (once per year). Towing the boat long distances with the shrouds tied on the mast and through the spreaders will fatigue them at spreader height. File off any sharp edges

where the shroud passes through the spreader.

Problem 4. Mast breaking on the bottom when capsized

Solutions

a. Don't capsize in shallow water!

b. If you do capsize in shallow water stop the boat inverting by getting straight onto the centreboard.

The Boom

Compared to the mast the boom is simple. It should be as light as possible while being strong enough not to break or over-bend. Carbon is an excellent material to use although most class rules will specify

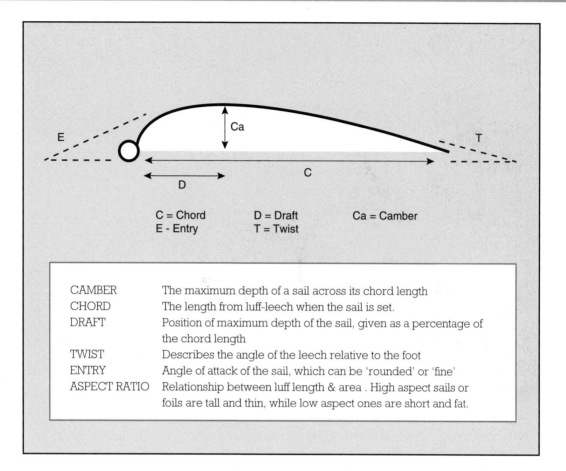

C = Chord   D = Draft   Ca = Camber
E - Entry   T = Twist

CAMBER	The maximum depth of a sail across its chord length
CHORD	The length from luff-leech when the sail is set.
DRAFT	Position of maximum depth of the sail, given as a percentage of the chord length
TWIST	Describes the angle of the leech relative to the foot
ENTRY	Angle of attack of the sail, which can be 'rounded' or 'fine'
ASPECT RATIO	Relationship between luff length & area . High aspect sails or foils are tall and thin, while low aspect ones are short and fat.

aluminium and even provide an exact section.

Fittings

The outhaul should have sufficient purchase and little friction.

The vang fitting must be strong as this is the most common cause of boom failure. It should preferably spread the load as much as possible.

If allowed in the class rules it is a good idea to cut away the end of the boom as it will make it lighter and will keep it clear of the water should you heel over. This could even prevent a careless capsize.

THE SAILS

Sails are the driving force of any high-performance boat and sail technology continues to develop rapidly with new materials, new designs and entirely new processes. All of these have enabled sails to be lighter and hold their shape better.

How is sail shape described?

Around your club you may hear all kinds of different expresions for describing sail shape. "This sail has plenty of belly!", "This one's got a tight leech" etc. The list above gives the definitive terminology for describing the shape of your sails.

Checking the tension in the mainsail's battens.

How a sail is designed and constructed

Most sail design and manufacture is now computor aided (CAD & CAM).
A mould is created on the computer to determine the shape and dimensions of the sail which can then be run through a stress/flow program to evaluate the stresses on the sail. If the applied loads change the sail beyond its desired flying shape then the procces is re-run until the desired flying shape is achieved. Smoothness and shape are viewed on the computer screen and the panel layout is selected. The panels are then nested for efficient cloth consumption when being cut by the laser cutter. The sail is then computer cut and ready for assembly.

The relationship between broadseam & luff curve

Most sails are shaped using a combination of broadseam and luff curve.

What is broadseam?
Normally the top edge of each panel is curved and the bottom edge is straight. When the sail is being constructed the curved top edge is stuck to the straight underside of the next panel, forcing in shape. This is called broadseam and is a shape fixed into the sail - it cannot be removed however much you bend your mast. Large amounts of broadseam are found in small dinghy sails which do not carry too much mast bend, e.g. the Enterprise, 420 etc..

What is luff curve?
The curve built into the luff of the sail forces shape into the sail when set on the mast. This shape, unlike broadseam, can be removed by bending the mast.

Most high-performance boats have very pre-bent masts and therefore have sails with lots of luff curve. Having less broadseam enables the sailor to bend the mast to de-power the rig and reduces drag. It is the combination of the amount of luff curve and broadseam that makes a good all-round sail.

Sail-cloth is a key factor in making the sail work efficiently and varies substantially depending on the type of boat.

The two most important considerations are stretch and weight. Most conventional classes use Dacron, a woven cloth with relatively poor stretch qualities. Most new high-performance classes sail with higher loads and opt for lower stretch cloths to help maintain the correct flying shape. These are often in the form of laminates such as Mylar which offer good stretch characteristics in all directions but can sometimes be hard to read in lighter airs, particularly when used on headsails.

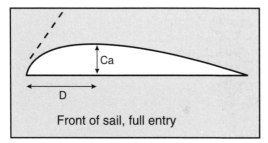

Front of sail, full entry

Pull down on the jib tack and the depth moves forward, making the entry full.

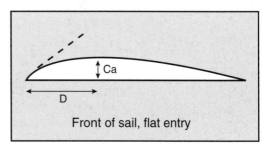

Front of sail, flat entry

Ease up on the jib tack and the entry becomes progressively flatter.

Pull the adjuster tight for heavy airs - note how the camber is pulled forward.

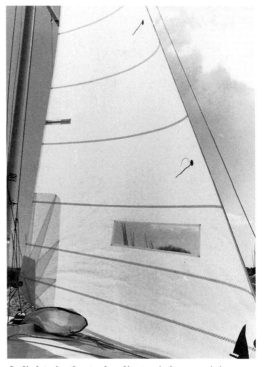

In light air, the tack adjuster is loose, giving a flat entry, with wrinkles at the luff.

All sails degrade with use and looking after the sails extends their competitive life considerably.

- Never fold your sails unless it's absolutely essential. (Of course, you'll have to fold the spinnaker).

- Try to avoid letting your sails flap unless it's absolutely unavoidable, because this breaks down the cloth (especially laminated cloth).

- Try to wash off salt, and dry wet sails.

- Repair minor rips/holes before they deteriorate.

- Do not leave your jib furled for long periods of time (especially in strong UV).

Fully-battened sails

Full length battens are now commonplace in the dinghy and small keelboat world. They not only support the larger roaches of modern sails, but improve the longevity of sails by stopping them flapping They also allow camber to be altered by batten tension. Tightening the battens will increase depth and tighten the leech, while loosening the battens will do the opposite. For the battens to work correctly you should push them in with uniform tension. Having your battens in too

Ease up the jibsheet leads to twist the leech in very light or strong winds.

Pull the jibsheet leads down to increase power and pointing ability in medium winds.

tight can hinder your light air performance. Always check your battens before hoisting the sail.

Batten stiffness

Batten stiffness can greatly affect the shape of the sail.

Top Tornado sailors change their battens for different weather and even take two sets on the water (taped along the boom).
Stiffer battens flatten the sail, open the leech and help to stop backwinding (drag). Softer battens give less support, increase the depth and tighten the leech . If you have a choice within your class rules we suggest you start by consulting your sailmaker.

SAIL CONTROLS

To achieve the best from a particular set of sails a number of controls are used to govern the shape.

Mainsail controls

Outhaul
The outhaul controls the depth in the lower third of the sail. Loosening will make the sail deeper. Tightening will flatten it off.

Cunningham
The cunningham affects the draft postion of the sail and the upper leech profile. More tension pulls the draft forwards and twists open the top of the sail.

Vang/kicking strap
The vang controls the leech profile of the mainsail and the overall depth through its effect on mastbend.

Jib controls

Luff tension (jib cunningham)
Like the mainsail cunnigham, this affects the draft postion and upper leech profile of the jib. More tension pulls the draft forwards and opens the upper leech. As a general rule apply enough tension to just remove the creases running at 90 degrees from the luff. Having too little jib cunningham will make the entry very fine and can make the jib hard to steer to. (The higher the wind strength the tighter the luff tension should be). See pictures on page 33.

Jib sheeting angle
Along with the sheet tension the jib sheeting angle determines the depth and leech profile of the jib.

Jib halyard tension
Affects the depth , draft postion & angle of entry.
If you find that it is hard to read the jib in very light airs then try sailing with less rig tension as this will round the front of the jib making steering easier (good in the Laser 5000).

Spinnaker controls

Halyard tension
This affects the luff length of the asymmetric. You don't always need to pull the head right up to the mast as this can overtighten the luff.

Twinning lines
These can be used to change the profile of the leech in much the same way as jib leads affect the sheeting angle of the jib.

Calibration

It is important that all your major rig and sail controls are well calibrated to enable you to reproduce fast settings. It is also a good idea to record your settings in a book for future reference.

What you need from your sailmaker

Strict one-design sailors only have to decide when their sails need replacing, but in classes with 'open' sails pay careful consideration when selecting your sailmaker.

- Have the sails got a good track record?

- Do they suit your mast section?

- Does the sailmaker have good tuning information?

- Have the sails only been succesful in particular conditions?

- Do the sails only perform with a particular crew weight?

If the sailmaker can anwser all these questions satifactorily you can go ahead with your purchase. If not then look elsewhere!

One of the biggest mistakes sailors make is buying cheap sails and not the best available at the time. While this is very tempting in the short term it can lead to a lack of performance and a great waste of time and effort.

THE CREW

Compatibility
Nothing is more divisive in a racing boat than a personality clash between helm and crew. For a partnership to work successfully it is important that you not only get on and can have fun sailing together, but that you have enough mutual respect not to start blaming

each other when things go wrong. In high-performance boats you are very dependent on your partner and you must develop a sense of team.

Weight
Many boats now feature weight equalisation but for those that don't crew weight is a big issue. It is important to be the right weight for the boat as you cannot afford to be exposed at either end of the wind range. In single-trapeze boats it is also a benefit to have as much of the team weight on the trapeze as possible. If you are not the perfect weight for the class it is not always the end of the world as proven by the range of crew/helm weights that has been successful in many Olympic classes. The key thing is not to let it affect you mentally.

Physical fitness
(See the Fernhurst book: *Mental & Physical Fitness for Sailing*)
Physical fitness in itself may never win you a race, but a lack of fitness will certainly contribute to your losing races. The amount of training needed is a highly individual and class-orientated requirement. Only you can tell if you are fit enough to race your boat hard enough to achieve your goals. Do you feel as fresh in the last race of a series as you did in the first?

The shorter courses that are increasingly being used for high-performance racing place different demands on our bodies. The stamina needed for the traditional two- or three-hour race is being replaced by a need for agility, aerobic fitness, speed and quick reactions. That is not to say that we no longer need any stamina, as anybody who has sailed several short course races back-to-back will vouch.

Here are the two easiest ways to maintain or improve your physical performance:

1. For aerobic fitness try regular running,

TOP TIPS: FOOD

 Drink plenty of water all the time

 Eat carboydrate immediately after exercise, eg sandwiches, pasta, bananas, potatoes, peas, beans.

 Have breakfast 3-4 hours before the start: cereal, toast and orange juice are ideal. A fried breakfast is not.

 Before the race have a sandwich, cereal bar and carbohydrate drink.

 Drink fluid between races.

swimming, cycling or any other physical sport that you enjoy (40 min duration 3 times/week).

2. Stretching. This should always be carried out before and after exercise (including sailing) as it plays a major role not only in improving flexibility, but also preventing injury.

FOOD AND DRINK

It is important that you eat and drink well to give your body the fuel it needs to operate at its best. Good sources of carbohydrate (eg breakfast cereals, bread, potatoes, pasta, rice) are essential to maintain your energy levels for competition and should be taken as soon after exercise as possible. While afloat it is simply not practical to eat many of the items listed above. It is often easier to replenish your carbohydrate store with a fluid carbohydrate drink. These come in the form of powders that can be mixed with a drink of your choice.

Fluid intake is as important as carbohydrate. As little as 2% dehydration will cause fatigue and affect both performance and judgement. To avoid dehydration you must try to drink before, during and after training and racing.

What should you drink?
A variety of drinks are good for rehydration (eg water, isotonic mixes and most soft drinks). Try to avoid tea, coffee and alcohol, all of which dehydrate you.

How much should you drink?
This will depend on the climate, your physique, clothing and work rate. As a rough guide you should be passing urine regularly and its colour should be pale or clear. If you feel thirsty you have usually left it too late and you are already becoming dehydrated.

MENTAL FITNESS

People who are mentally strong have a tremendous advantage over competitors who are not. This subject is well covered in *Mental and Physical Fitness for Sailing*, but here are the key qualities required to win

1. Controlled aggression

2. Self-belief.

3. Patience.

4. Durability (never give up).

5. Good concentration.

The pecking order phenomenon

In sailing more than most sports people get used to the normal 'pecking order' in fleet racing. There is no God given reason why the same people should be at the front of the fleet. It is fundamental to our mental approach that we believe somebody has got to win and it might as well be us!

Clothing

Good sailors need good clothing to perform well. Good clothing must provide

1. Correct temperature during and between races.

2. Good feel.

3. Good grip.

4. Good flexibility.

5. Good protection.

6. Comfort.

PART TWO
BOATHANDLING

2 BOATHANDLING

The trend towards shorter courses and faster boats demands an increasing emphasis on boathandling skills. Competitors are continually refining their boathandling, both to gain an advantage and also in response to the quirks that every new design of boat appears to display. It is interesting to find more than one solution to any given problem; for instance a particularly light crew may approach things in a different way to a heavier, stronger crew.

Good boathandling – the foundation for winning.

How good must your boathandling be?

The first level to reach is where you can carry out the major boathandling elements satisfactorily. Next, you should aim to be able to race around a course tidily and without any disasters. But the race winning crews will be

A light air tack. Head up slowly, heeling the boat to leeward slightly.

The crew and helmsman roll the boat together. The mainsheet is pulled in to help the turn. The tiller is used to increase the turn rate.

The crew backs the jib slightly. N the weight is kept forward to kee, the transom out.

one level higher. They are able to react well under pressure from other boats and are able to adapt what they are doing to an ever-changing environment. These crews are really in control of their boats and are not letting their boathandling dictate their race tactics. When you get to this stage your boathandling can start to be considered good enough.

How to get better fast

The nice thing about boathandling is that practice tends to make perfect and most people can reach a high standard through putting in some concerted effort. To improve rapidly always discuss what you are trying to achieve and where things are going wrong. Only then can you make the changes to get better. It is well worth watching people in the fleet who are better than you noting exactly what they do. If in doubt ask them how they do things - winners love to tell everyone how good they are and how they do it! A final point to note is that boathandling under pressure is a whole different game from boathandling on your own.

Try to simulate pressure situations when you are practising. You may find the drills in Fernhurst Books' *Race Training* of use during your training sessions.

TACKING

The new designs of boat are slower to tack for several reasons.

1. The boats are light and don't carry their momentum easily. They do however accelerate quickly.

2. The upwind planing hulls slow considerably when they come off the plane. A fast boat will always lose more distance when seconds are wasted tacking.

3. The large fully-battened mainsails create more drag than a soft sail and are often hard to flick over to the new tack.

e helmsman eases the mainsheet)ear away on the new tack. e jib is brought across but not •eted hard.

The helmsman and crew pull the boat up together, keeping their weight forward. The sails are squeezed in together.

The tack is completed. The sails are at their optimum trim.

Light air tacking: common mistakes. If you turn too sharply the rudder acts as a brake.

Over-rolling stalls the foils and can cause a capsize.

Over-rolling after the tack is also slow.

Single wire tacking.

Unless you are confident in your ability to tack you will be reluctant to tack on windshifts and will suffer tactically.

Tacking in light airs

In light airs you need to roll tack the boat, both to help her turn and to fan the rig upright to accelerate on the new tack. The most common faults are:

1. Rolling the boat to windward too early (makes luffing up harder and encourages the crew to pull the boat up too early).

2. Turning the boat too sharply (the rudder acts as a brake).

3. Not flicking the battens to the new tack. (Rolling the boat upright and pumping the main normally does this as long as there is some leech tension via the vang - if the boom skies they might not flick across.)

4. Over-rolling the boat. This can cause the boat's racks/wings to dig into the water, water to be scooped into the cockpit, or a near capsize as the weight and momentum of a large fully-battened rig comes over.

5. Over-sheeting the jib or mainsail out of the tack when trying to accelerate.

6. Sitting too far back in the boat and digging the transom in.
   The key word to emphasise when roll tacking is 'rhythm' as any vigorous action will slow the boat down. If something goes wrong and momentum is lost the key to accelerating is to bear away slightly and ease the sheets to twist open the leeches of the sails.

Single wire tacking

Tacking is relatively easy in light/medium winds with just the crew on the trapeze, because the water is normally still flat, the battens flick across

Twin-trapeze tracking.

easily and there is enough wind to accelerate quickly on the new tack. The main priority is for the crew to have a good technique so he can cross the boat quickly and yet smoothly. He needs to be able to tack from one trapeze to the other while tending to the jib accurately.

The helmsman must turn the boat smoothly and trim the mainsail to keep the boat flat to help the crew come into and out of the tack, while smoothly crossing the boat in time with the crew.

- Begin with the boat flat and going fast.

- The helmsman then luffs gently. The crew takes his weight on his forward hand and unhooks from the trapeze.

- Continue to turn, with the mainsheet still trimmed in to assist the turn.

- As the boat approaches head-to-wind, turn a little more sharply and let the boat roll to windward. The crew uncleats the jib and backs it momentarily with one hand to help the turn, while picking up the new jibsheet in his other hand.

- Coming out of the tack the helmsman slows the rate of turn and the crew starts to pull in the jib. Both stay on their toes, to be fast and agile, and move together.

- The helmsman swaps hands on the mainsheet and tiller. The crew grabs the trapeze handle in his forward hand and starts to move out, while still pulling the jib in smoothly with his aft hand.

- The helmsman hikes hard and plays the mainsheet to keep the boat flat. The crew puts his full weight on the wire and finishes trimming the jib.

- Settle down quickly, and go!

Common faults

1. Heeling too far to leeward before the tack, caused either by the crew coming in too early or by the helmsman failing to luff enough as the crew comes in. Ideally you don't want to ease the mainsheet because keeping the main in helps the boat luff.

2. Heeling too far to leeward out of the tack caused by the helmsman not easing the sheet as required. This will tire the crew who cannot swing out but must climb out as the boat is heels over. The rudder will load up and the boat won't accelerate.

3. Turning too sharply and stopping the boat.

4. Backing the jib for too long, which stops the boat and makes it heel and/or capsize.

Twin-trapeze tacking

For the crew, twin-trapeze tacking is similar to single-trapeze tacking, except he has to be more aware of the helmsman's movements in case the helmsman wants to slow down or speed up the tack. The helmsman has not only to learn to get from one trapeze to the other, but also to steer accurately and control the power with the mainsail.

- Preparing to tack, the helmsman and crew tidy their sheets.

- As the boat heads up and the power comes out of the rig the helmsman moves in, back foot first, slightly ahead of the crew who has unhooked from his trapeze.

- The helmsman slides his hand down the tiller extension and unhooks with his mainsheet hand.

- Passing head-to-wind helmsman and crew cross the boat together. The crew uncleats the jib and picks up the new jibsheet in his other hand. The helmsman continues to turn smoothly.

- Completing the tack, the crew moves fast to balance the boat, grabbing the handle with his front hand and pulling the jib in with his back hand as he goes. The helmsman grabs the tiller with the hand holding the mainsheet, then hooks on with his free hand (the old tiller hand).

- Once hooked on, the helmsman can take the mainsheet in his forward hand and swing out onto the trapeze, sliding his hand along the tiller extension as he goes and pulling in the mainsheet to support their combined weight.

- Finally, with the tack complete, the crew hooks on.

Common faults

1. Cleating the mainsail which will cause the boat to heel if there is a gust.

2. Sitting down or kneeling.

3. Coming into the boat too early and letting it heel to leeward.

4. Letting the boat heel to leeward out of the tack (ideally it should be heeling slightly to windward, then as you swing out with the sheet it will accelerate fast).

5. Not steering accurately and smoothly (this is the hardest part, as your body has to move through quite a distance without affecting the angle of the tiller).

6. If you have the vang hard on there is always a danger that you may get stuck head-to-wind with a fully-battened mainsail.

TOP TIP

The helmsman can practice trapeze tacking by getting the crew to sit in the boat and furl the jib or leave it flapping. The helmsman can then swing around, practising his tacks at will with the crew watching and offering advice. Concentrate on working out the best footwork and repeating the tack over and over until it is second nature.

How not to bear away. The boat is heeled, the jib is pinned in, crew weight is forward. Note the angle of the tiller, rudder turbulence and the bow in deep.

With the weight back and the boat flatter, the boat bears away smoothly with less tiller movement. Note the crew is unhooked but pulling hard on the trapeze handle and the helmsman is still hiking hard.

Tips for tacking in survival weather

1. When there are very big waves the helmsman may have to come in and sit on the side prior to the tack because there is otherwise too high a risk of capsizing.

2. In windy weather it is safer for the crew to uncleat the jib while he's still on the trapeze as the helmsman calls the tack, because any backing of the jib may capsize the boat. Easing the jib before the tack also helps the boat luff up, particularly when it is very windy and the mainsail is well eased.

BEARING AWAY IN HEAVY AIR

It's not easy to bear away from the wind onto a downwind leg in lots of wind in a high-performance boat with a powerful fully-battened mainsail, particularly if both helm and crew are trapezing. The main problem is that you need to keep the boat flat or, preferably, heeled to windward. So your weight needs to be out, in order to 'pull away', and yet once you have borne off you need to move your weight in quickly to prevent wiping out to windward. There is also a considerable increase in speed and a high risk of nosediving. There are several key factors for succeeding in this manoeuvre

1. Ease the vang to de-power the mainsail (especially in the top).

2. Leave the cunningham hard on until you have borne away.

3. Move your weight right back in the boat to lift the bow.

4. The crew must uncleat the jib and unhook from the trapeze (holding the handle).

5. Bear away onto a broad reach easing the sails as you go. Once the turn is safely under way the crew can move into the boat.

6. If he needs to, the helmsman should come in back-foot-first once things are more under control.

SPINNAKER WORK

As high-performance boats get faster and faster downwind, particularly with asymmetric spinnakers, any seconds saved by slick spinnaker work translate into more and more distance gained. Equally, mistakes are punished hard.

Conventional spinnakers

The basic routine of hoisting, gybing and dropping conventional spinnakers has been extensively written about in the past and is clearly explained in both *Helming to Win* and *Crewing to Win* from Fernhurst Books. We will concentrate on the asymmetric.

ASYMMETRIC SPINNAKERS

An asymmetric spinnaker is essentially a large genoa made of lightweight cloth flown from a bowsprit that normally retracts for upwind work. These sails are far easier to trim and gybe than conventional spinnakers, but their size can make handling difficult.

Rigging

Rigging the asymmetric can be confusing particularly if the boat has a chute and a downhaul. Here are some rigging tips.

1. It is always easier to rig the spinnaker with the bowsprit out (this also ensures the bowsprit will not roll over and twist the tack of the sail).

2. Label the three corners (head, tack and clew) to save time and embarrassing mistakes.

3. First tie the tack, then work along the luff and tie the head to the halyard. Tie the clew next,

Tie the tack tight to the bowsprit, except in light winds.

Work up the luff and attach the head. Then work down the leech and attach the clew.

Fix the sheets to the clew with a small knot.

having worked down the leech checking for twists, and then worry about the downhaul if there is one.

4. When you have a downhaul remember the motto 'the sheet goes over the downhaul'.

5. Avoid tying the sheets to the clew with large knots as they will then catch on the jib luff when gybing and dropping.

6. Always double-check that the halyard is not twisted around the jib luff and that the kite is the correct side of the jibsheets, shrouds, lowers, etc.

7. Tie the tack as close to the bowsprit as possible or the spinnaker will fall off to leeward. N.B. In light winds do not tie the tack too tight to the bowsprit as it can affect how the sail sets just off the pole.

8. Always tape up the bow fittings and head of the jib to avoid ripping the spinnaker.

Chute v bag

Chutes

Spinnaker chutes are very simple to use on both hoists and drops, but the bigger the sail the harder it is to pull into the chute. Chutes also tend to break down the fabric of the sail. If the jib is mounted on the bow and the spinnaker has to be pulled into a chute on one side of the jib, you must decide which side to rig the spinnaker.

In the International 14 with port-hand roundings we set up the spinnaker on the left side of the jib as we nearly always hoist on starboard tack. We make the drop easier by either coming into the leeward mark on starboard (leeward drop) or by running very low on the drop to let the spinnaker float to windward of the jib. Others choose to have a more awkward hoist but drop on port tack at the leeward mark.

If the jib tack is mounted behind the chute, choice of side is not an issue as the spinnaker always comes down in front of the jib.

Bags

Because of the size of most asymmetric spinnakers, bags are often preferred despite the extra work it entails for the crew. The main disadvantage of bags is that it will normally take longer to drop the spinnaker as it has to be gathered by hand. In conventional spinnaker boats hoisting from the windward bag must be done with care as the spinnaker must be thrown forward of the jib luff to stop it blowing back through the jib slot. This is not the case in asymmetric spinnaker boats because:

1. Pulling the bowsprit out pulls the kite forward and stops it blowing through the jib slot.

2. With asymmetrics you have to sail fairly low at the moment you hoist to prevent getting blown over, and you don't lose much by running slightly lower to help the spinnaker blow round the front.
   Windward hoists onto a run are very often faster as there is no friction against the jib.

Hoisting the asymmetric

Every boat is set up slightly differently in terms of how the bowsprit outhaul and the spinnaker halyard are led in the boat, but they fall into three main categories.

a. Both ropes are led so that only the crew can use them.

b. Both are led so that the helm or crew can use them.

c. The bowsprit is automatically pulled out as the halyard is pulled up, the halyard being led to the crew.

Hoisting an asymmetric. Pull out the bowsprit.

Pull up the spinnaker. (On some boats one rope pulls the sail up and the pole out.)

Pull in the leeward sheet.

The routine

It is essentially very simple!

1. Take the slack out of the leeward spinnaker sheet and make sure the windward one will run free (this can be done going upwind, before the weather mark).

2. Pull the bowsprit out as far as it will go (mark the rope clearly).

3. Pull the spinnaker to the top of the mast (mark the rope clearly).

4. Grab the leeward spinnaker sheet and go!

Note that some boats are different. The 49er, for example, has one rope which both pulls up the spinnaker and pulls out the pole.

When getting used to this it is easiest for the helmsman to concentrate on steering accurately and keeping the boat upright and for the crew to do all the work. (In twin-wire boats this can mean the helmsman staying on the trapeze if necessary.) The helmsmen can speed things up by pulling in the leeward sheet as the crew completes the hoist.

When you are comfortable with the handling of a category B boat it will actually be faster

Here the chase boat follows us round the buoy and through a hoist. As you approach, check the spinnaker sheets and decide on a straight or a gybe set.

Keep your weight out to bear away neatly.

As the crew pulls out the bowsprit the helmsman steers with one knee while resting on the other and hoisting the spinnaker with two hands.

for the helmsman to pull up the spinnaker on a run, while the crew does the bowsprit and is ready to sheet in as soon as the spinnaker is right up. This is particularly effective in trapeze boats because the crew can jump straight out on the wire with the spinnaker sheet to balance as it fills. To pull up the spinnaker quickly the helmsman will need both hands and will have to cleat the mainsheet and steer with one knee while kneeling on the other for stability. In light winds it may be possible to stand up and steer with your knees. Be careful to steer accurately and low during the hoist.

Hoisting onto a tight reach

It is important to keep sailing high as the spinnaker is pulled up, both to protect your wind and to give the fastest angle to the next mark. To do this the helmsman should continue trapezing/hiking while the crew hoists the spinnaker. You will however have to bear off as the spinnaker fills to avoid getting blown over. Leave the cunningham on and let off the vang to depower the mainsail and enable you to sail higher with less risk of getting blown over.

Gybing

Gybing an asymmetric is very simple. Unlike a conventional spinnaker it is far easier and there is no difference between reach-to-reach gybing and run-to-run gybing.

Helmsman's routine

1. Get the boat up to maximum speed to take the pressure off the rig.

2. Turn the boat smoothly and pull the boom over with the mainsheet system as the boat's stern passes through the eye of the wind.

3. As the boom fills on the new side pull the tiller to straighten up. (If it's very windy you may have to turn back down onto a run as the sails refill.)

4. Change hands, hike out and head up. Sail higher than normal to accelerate to full speed.

5. Resume normal sailing angles (See Part 3).

Crew's routine

1. Make sure the spinnaker sheets are not tangled (or under your feet).

As the spinnaker fills the helmsman and crew move to balance the boat.

Make sure the boat is at full speed before gybing.

As the helmsman starts to bear away, helmsman and crew come in off the trapeze.

The crew keeps the old spinnaker sheet in to prevent twist.

2. If you are trapezing, unhook and come into the boat as it bears away.

3. Uncleat the jib.

4. Hold on to the old spinnaker sheet or even pull it in a touch until the boat is on a run, then pull the new sheet in as fast as possible as you cross the boat. If you release the old sheet too early or fail to pull in the new sheet fast enough the spinnaker will twist.

5. Once the spinnaker fills on the new side you will need to ease some sheet for optimum trim. Oversheeting kills your boatspeed.

6. Trim the jib on the new side.

7. Hook on and get out on the trapeze.

Differences in light airs

1. It will pay to roll gybe by heeling the boat to windward as you bear away, then fan the sails as you pull it upright on the new tack. (Be careful not to over-roll as you may fill with water, dig in a wing or even capsize if the rig is big and heavy.)

2. You may need some vang tension (take up slack) to hold a bit of leech tension and help flick the battens across.

3. Turn off the ratchets to help the spinnaker sheet pay out. (If it is lead to the back of the boat the helmsman can sometimes

A good roll gybe spoiled by the top batten not flicking across. This was caused by our gybing with no vang on. But note the helmsman steering with his knees and keeping the spinnaker full.

e helmsman pulls the boom over d the crew pulls in the new sheet.

The crew eases the sheet as it fills and moves onto the trapeze. The helmsman swaps hands, hooks on and moves out onto the trapeze.

The helmsman heads up to accelerate and sheets in the main. Once at full speed he resumes the best VMG (Velocity Made Good) angle.

feed it out.)

4. You can turn the boat much quicker, as you will be sailing higher angles and will have further to turn.

5. You can pre-set the jib by pulling the windward jibsheet in and uncleating the leeward jibsheet before gybing. If you have a furler it is a good idea to furl the jib downwind.

Twin-trapeze gybing

Agile helmsmen should gybe in a similar way to twin-trapeze tacking.

1. Start to turn gently.

2. Come in, stand up and unhook with your mainsheet hand.

3. Pull the main over facing forwards, duck under the boom and straighten up.

4. Swap your hands on tiller and mainsheet, hook on and swing out on the new side, heading up and taking the mainsheet with you.

You should aim to do all this in one continuous movement and always stay on your feet. In survival weather you will probably not be twin trapezing, but if you are, come in first and then gybe as for a single-trapeze boat. Less agile helmsmen may be happier gybing like this in all wind strengths. Remember to turn the boat gently, as turning fast at high speed will result in swimming lessons.

Swinging bowsprits

If you have a bowsprit that can be pulled to windward, uncleat it as you turn into the gybe and pull it to windward as soon as possible afterwards. Remember that as you pull the pole to windward the crew will have to ease some sheet or the spinnaker will be oversheeted.

'Outside gybe'

On some boats, particularly ones with a short bowsprit like the Melges 24, there may hardly be room to flip the spinnaker through between the jib luff and spinnaker luff and it may be better to gybe it around the outside. This means tying the spinnaker sheet around the spinnaker luff and letting the sail fly round the front as you gybe. The problems with this are that you have lots of sheet to pull in, and there is a danger that the sheet can catch under the bowsprit. But this sort of gybe is much safer on keelboats with asymmetrics when it is very windy.

This sportsboat has a swinging bowsprit which enables the helmsman to sail lower.

Spinnaker drops

Chute

With a chute the spinnaker drop is easy. The crew simply uncleats the halyard and pole and pulls the spinnaker down as quickly as possible so that it doesn't fall into the water. Take care that neither the bowsprit outhaul nor the halyard re-cleat and that none of these ropes or the sheets jam, as these will stop the spinnaker coming in.

Bag

With a bag the spinnaker must be dropped to windward in dinghies in all but the lightest airs, so the crew must come in and pull it to windward of the jib. It is better to uncleat the pole first and gather the foot before letting the halyard go and bundling the spinnaker down into the bag. This is hard work for the crew when it is windy and the spinnaker is big, so you must allow plenty of time. Again, take care that the pole outhaul, halyard and sheet don't jam or re-cleat.

Preparing to drop, the crew passes the spinnaker sheet to the helmsman.

The helmsman bears off as the crew comes in and tightens the outhaul, lowers the centreboard, opens the bag, etc.

The crew pulls the windward sheet and starts to gather the spinnaker

WHAT DO YOU DO IF THE SPINNAKER TWISTS?

1. Pull hard on the sheet and try to free it.

2. Ease the halyard a bit to see if this helps the twist spin out.

3. Gybe back. This will normally untwist it.

4. Lower the spinnaker, being careful to not let it go in the water, and the crew can then untwist it by hand.

Dropping with a chute the crew simply uncleats the pole and halyard and pulls in the sail ASAP.

However you drop, the crew should pass the spinnaker sheet to the helmsman as he moves in to drop the spinnaker, as it can then be kept flying for an extra couple of seconds while the crew gets into position. If you have left the drop a bit late simply let the sheet go to slow down. While it may seem that the helmsman has little to do, he can help by talking to the crew and pointing out anything that is caught. It is also helpful to tell the crew how far from the mark you are as you approach it, so he can get ready to pull in the jib and swing onto the trapeze if necessary. The helmsman should be balancing the boat with his weight and steering and preparing the boat for the beat (cunningham, mainsheet strops, kicker etc).

Better safe than sorry!
The distance lost by not getting the spinnaker down in time and doing a poor leeward mark

...anwhile the helmsman balances ...boat.

The crew finishes packing the kite and the helmsman starts to head up.

With the spinnaker packed the crew can rejoin the helmsman on the wire.

The gybe drop. Get set to gybe.   *Gybe as normal.*   *The crew pulls the 'old' spinnak*
sheet hard.

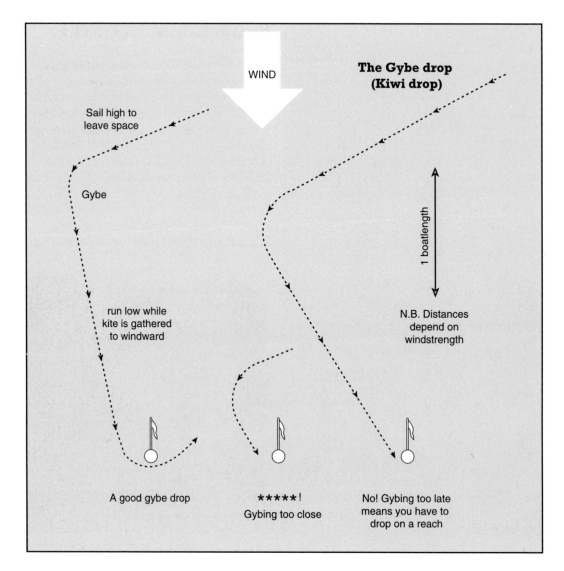

helmsman steers low as the
w gathers in the spinnaker.

The crew tidies up as the helmsman
starts to head up.

The crew sheets in the jib and gets
ready to go out on the wire.

rounding is far greater than anything lost by
taking it down too early, so if in doubt drop
early! Always get the outhaul on and
centreboard down before dropping as these
are both hard to do after the mark.

'Kiwi' or gybe drop

If you need to gybe to drop at the leeward mark
you should approach a few boatlengths high of
the layline and gybe above the mark. By holding
on to the old sheet and not easing it, the
spinnaker will end up to windward of the jib and
ready to be gathered into the bag as above.

360 AND 720 TURNS

With a 360 turn allowed to exonerate hitting a
mark and a 720 turn often allowed as an
alternative penalty, there is a fairly high chance
that you will end up sailing in circles from time
to time, especially if you are racing hard against
close fleets over small courses. With a bit of
boathandling practice this need not be a total
disaster if you follow these rules.

1. Don't panic.

2. Ease the vang and warn your crew.

The crew is passing the spinnaker sheet to the helmsman prior to moving inboard to drop the kite.

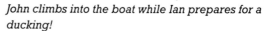

The San Francisco Roll. With the mast into the wind be prepared for the boat to flip.

John climbs into the boat while Ian prepares for a ducking!

Will she stabilise?

****! As the boat capsizes again, John climbs over joins Ian on the daggerboard.

3. Work out whether it is best to tack first or gybe. Normally it is best to gybe first downwind and tack first upwind, but this depends on the situation and wind strength.

4. Turn neatly, heeling the boat and trimming the sails to assist the turn. Do not turn too sharply and fill up with water.

5. After doing the penalty forget it, settle down and start to catch up.

6. Remember that while exonerating yourself you have no right of way – so keep your eyes open!

CAPSIZING!

As high-performance boats get faster and have bigger sail plans capsizing will be more common. Unlike the old designs, most new boats are self-draining and a capsize is not terminal if handled correctly – after all if it is windy enough for you to capsize, others probably will too.

In the 1993 Prince of Wales Cup Chris Fox and Ian were leading by 200 metres when they capsized at the last turning mark. Having capsized many times in practice they had worked out the best technique and were able to right the boat quickly. They were disappointed to lose the lead

a breath.

Glug! Ian is under the boat, holding the daggerboard
and slowing down the 'flip'.

the mast downwind, the boat can be righted
:ly.

Maximise your weight like this.

When getting blown over to leeward the helmsman and crew unhook and try to save a capsize by
pulling on the trapeze wires.

TOP TIPS

1. When capsized always ease the vang and drop the spinnaker if it's up.

2. One person (the nearest or heaviest) should always get on the centreboard as quickly as possible to stop the boat inverting. Do not hang onto the boat and pull it upside down.

3. If you get blown over to leeward and are on the trapeze try to unhook otherwise you will be pulled into the sails. This increases the chance of inverting and risks damaging the mainsail. If it is too late, try to jump clear of the mainsail or at least try your best to spread your weight on impact!

4. Don't waste time swimming around the boat if it is quicker to pull yourself under the gunwale and pop up the other side. (Try not to drown by getting tangled in ropes.)

5. Maximise your weight to pull the boat up quickly. One person hangs onto the boat or a rope, and the other pulls his body.

6. If the mast is into the wind and it is windy the boat will probably flip over and you should hang on to the centreboard either to stop it or to emerge still on the board as it re-capsizes (a San Francisco Roll).

7. If it is really rough you may need one person to swim the bow into the wind and waves.

If you're going to go, try to jump clear of the sails (helmsman) or spread your weight (crew).

and the cup but were pleased to get everything sorted out quickly and hang on to second place. Practising capsizing might sound funny, but it can win races.

Saving a leeward capsize

If you are being blown over to leeward you can often recover by unhooking from the trapeze and pulling on the trapeze ring, instead of getting pulled by the trapeze into the mainsail which always leads to a capsize.

PART THREE
TECHNIQUE AND
BOATSPEED

3 TECHNIQUE AND BOATSPEED

While the shorter courses and faster boats are making racing more boathandling orientated, boatspeed is still very important: 'Boatspeed makes you a tactical genius'. Good boatspeed will often give you an edge that takes the pressure off both your tactics and your boathandling. Slow boats rarely win races.

UPWIND

VERY LIGHT AIRS

In very light winds your first goal should be to keep the air flowing around the sails. This is primarily achieved by making sure they are not too full and, most importantly, that the leeches are open. This means easing the sheets and perhaps bending the mast or moving the jib leads back or up. These will both flatten the sails and open the leeches. Once you have got the boat moving and the flow 'attached to the sails' you can progressively sheet in and aim to point. As soon as the boat slows due to sailing too high, a bad wave or a bad tack, you will have to ease the sheets again to re-attach the flow.

Leech telltales can be used to detect whether the wind is flowing off the back of the sail or not, but fully-battened mainsails are generally very difficult to read and give few clues as to whether they are backwinded or not. You must be careful to not push all the battens in too tight, especially in the head, as these push fullness into the sail.

Trim and balance

Aim to sail the boat with the minimum wetted surface area, which means sitting well forward to lift the stern, and maybe heeling slightly to leeward. (Heeling too far to leeward will make the sails hard to read and will reduce the efficiency of both rig and foils.) Be careful not to sit in the slot and aim to sit down low in the boat.

Kinetics

Rocking, pumping, sculling, ooching and repeated tacking or gybing are prohibited, as is accelerating out of a tack faster than you would have been going without kinetics. Note that nearly all of these terms include the word 'repeated' in their definition, and you can often get away with the odd singular kinetic movement.

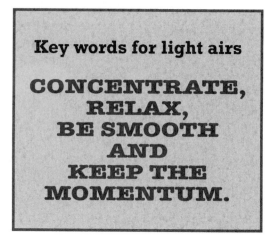

Key words for light airs

CONCENTRATE, RELAX, BE SMOOTH AND KEEP THE MOMENTUM.

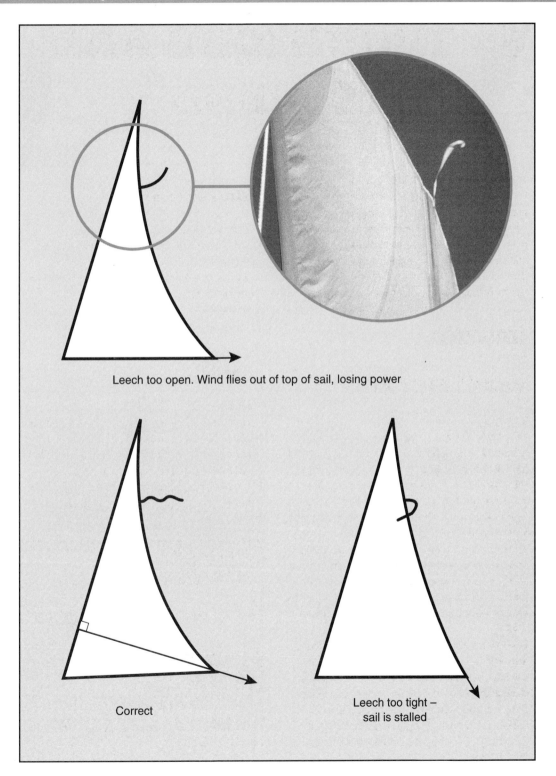

Leech too open. Wind flies out of top of sail, losing power

Correct

Leech too tight –
sail is stalled

CHECKLIST FOR LIGHT AIRS

Rake - upright (check your class norm and tuning sheet)

Rig tension - varies according to rig and sails(check the class norm)

Spreaders - normal position or swing them backwards to put some pre-bend in the mast. (Remember that as you rake the mast forwards for light winds it will straighten and sometimes invert for any given spreader setting.)

Uppers - Pulling these on can help to pre-bend the mast, but can make the rig feel too rigid and choked – try it and see.

Morrison wires - tighten to bend the mast and flatten the sail.

Lowers - ease to let the mast bend low down.

Strut - pull forward to bend the mast low down.

Mast chocks at deck level - should be neutral or chocked to pre-bend the mast low down.

Outhaul - reasonably tight, depending on cut of the sail.

Vang (kicking strap) - just take up the slack to help flick the battens in the tacks and gybes. Any tension will stall the leech.

Cunningham - fully eased.

Jib leads - moved back/up slightly to open the leech.

Centreboard - fully down and angled forwards if possible.

LIGHT/MEDIUM WINDS

In these conditions it is important to work hard for height. There is enough wind to keep the flow attached, and it is easy to get back up to speed by bearing off if you overdo it. There are also not too many waves to make you need to drive off lower to keep going. This means that you can sheet fairly hard on both mainsail and jib. If you slow too much simply bear off and momentarily open the leeches (by easing sheets), before coming back up. It is a mistake to try and trapeze too early, particularly for the helmsman in twin-trapeze boats, as this will cause a tendency to bear off to try and stay on the trapeze. If it's marginal wiring, trapeze very high so that you can move in and out easily and lower yourself in the gusts.

Make your sails deeper to gain power and help to hold the leeches tight so you can point high.

Trapeze very high in marginal conditions so you can move in and out easily.

The ideal shape will very much depend on the wave state, with flat water needing flatter sails and choppy water needing fuller sails and more twist. Every effort should be made to get the boom on or near the centreline.

Steering

To steer most accurately it can pay in this wind

Mainsail leech. 1.Too closed. 2.Too open. 3.Correct – for flat water. The leech is fairly closed, but open at the top to put the boat 'on its toes'.

strength to hold the tiller extension behind you at 90 degrees to the tiller.

Trim/balance

The boat should be kept dead flat, although it may pay to heel slightly to leeward to get through any awkward waves. This gives the helm more feel and makes sure you don't end up heeled to windward. The trim depends on the wave state as you can keep further forward in flat water. As a general rule sail to give the boat maximum waterline length.

The jib leech is too tight. The main will backwind, power will be lost and the boat will stop.

Better! the jib leech follows the shape of the mainsail.

The helmsman is checking the slot while the crew plays the mainsheet. Don't take too long - if the speed drops so will the apparent wind, and the slot will look closed.

In light/medium wind this Laser 4000 is being sailed flat and being trimmed for maximum waterline length.

CHECKLIST FOR LIGHT/MEDIUM WINDS

Rake - Keep the mast upright until you are fully powered, then consider raking it back slightly.

Rig tension - You should have quite a lot of rig tension to maintain a straight jib luff and give you the range to let it off if the wind increases.

Spreaders - Standard settings will be fine.

Uppers - Enough tension to support the top of the mast sideways, but not enough to force pre-bend into the mast.

Morrison wires - These can be fairly loose to help power up the mast.

Lowers - Tighten these to straighten the mast low down, depending on sail cut and wave state.

Strut - Same as the lowers. Perhaps start to retain the mast more.

Chocks - Retain the mast or even chock it back slightly.

Jib leads - These can be moved forward/down slightly and can be brought inboard in flat water to help you point.

Outhaul - Ease a bit in choppy water or if you're looking for power.

Vang (kicking strap) - Leech tension should be held by the mainsheet as the vang bends the mast. Keep enough tension in the vang to stop the boom skying in the gusts when you have to ease the mainsheet.

Cunningham - Don't use it until you are overpowered.

Centreboard - Keep fully down/forward.

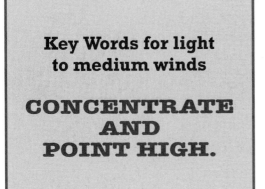

Key Words for light to medium winds	**Key Words for medium to strong winds**
CONCENTRATE AND POINT HIGH.	**WORK HARD AND FLAT IS FAST**

Kinetics

You shouldn't need kinetics in this weather.

MEDIUM/STRONG WINDS

It is in these winds that the greatest differences in angles occur between boats sailing upwind trying to gain the best VMG.

'Stab and flap' v 'Flow and go'

The dilemma is whether to foot off and play the sails continually to go fast through the water and generate good lift from the foils, or to sail high and de-power by feathering the boat up into the wind in the gusts. There is no correct answer because it depends on the boat, sail shape, your sailing technique and crew weight. In general light crews will have to feather more whereas heavy crews can pin the boat down, work hard and drive off. It will also pay more to foot when it is choppy as the 'stab and flappers' will simply get stopped by the waves.

In twin-trapeze boats it is far easier to 'stab and flap' as it's hard to play large amounts of mainsheet continually. Try not to get too obsessed with either method and sail high most

of the time, occasionally bringing the boat off the breeze slightly to get it moving really fast. High-performance boats should always be planing to windward in these conditions.

Trim and balance

You should be sailing the boat flat or in some cases heeled slightly to windward. This often works in twin-trapeze boats as the power and weight of the rig is kept right over the centre of resistance (the foils), and it gives better gust response because the boat does not heel to leeward immediately a puff hits you. You should be starting to move back in the boat slightly to encourage it to plane and to stop the bow hitting the waves. Always be ready to move forward again in the lulls or if there is a patch of flatter water.

Kinetics

The odd aggressive pump of the mainsail at the right moment might encourage the boat to pop onto the plane. This works well if it is combined with bearing off slightly to load up the rig. Both helmsman and crew should work very hard physically to keep the boat flat. Maximise weight on the trapeze by standing

CHECKLIST FOR
MEDIUM/STRONG WINDS

Rake - rake the mast back progressively as the wind increases. This is your main weapon for controlling the power and the other settings are based around it.

Rig tension - plenty of rig tension will prevent the jib luff sagging and will ensure the mast in twin-trapeze boats does not 'pop to windward' and break.

Spreaders - normal settings should be fine, although the further back you rake the more the mast will bend. This is good for de-powering, but don't overdo it or the mainsail will invert (large creases from spreaders to clew). If it does, move the spreaders forward.

Uppers - ease these off as you get more overpowered. This lets the topmast bend to leeward and allows the middle mast to come to windward slightly (when the uppers also pass through the lower spreaders). Be careful not to over-ease them or the mast will be vulnerable. Remember also to pull them on hard for the run or the asymmetric will break the top off the mast!

In the International 14 we found that easing the uppers let the mast "work" for us much more and made the boat easier to handle and much faster. We had a mark on the control beyond which we only dared go in times of dire need: if we were in a comfortable position we would only ease to the line. It is often said that masts are at their fastest just before they break!

Lowers - these can be eased slightly to let the mast bend low down. Don't forget though that as you rake back, these are effectively eased anyway.

Strut/chocks - same as the lowers. You might even have to retain the mast more, because of the effect of the rake.

Diamond wires - tighten them to prevent the mast inverting downwind.

Jib leads - these can be moved back to open the slot and de-power the jib, but remember that raking back does these things anyway. It can mean that you have to nudge them forward/down slightly, especially if the wind drops during the race and you can't change rake. If you stop pointing it's probably because the jib leech is too open.

Vang (kicking strap) - In general it pays to pull the vang on hard to bend the mast, flatten the mainsail, maintain some leech tension and make the mainsheet easier to play. Some boats, like the International 14, seem to respond to having little kicking strap tension and keeping the boom nearer the centreline. Experiment and see.

In the 470 we were once training in about 18 knots and quite a chop against the Italian Olympic representatives. We were going at similar speeds and decided John should get out and look at both rigs. As he swapped places with Derek Clark, our coach, John eased the vang. Derek didn't realise and left the vang eased and we lined up again against the Italians. This time we were consistently faster and remained so all day! (Easing the vang, was working in that boat with that rig in those particular conditions.)

Cunningham - this is a key control in these conditions, particularly with a fully-battened mainsail. It is important because it is easy to adjust and yet can transform the power of the rig and balance of the boat. In gusty conditions it should be adjusted continually, pulling lots on if you are overpowered and easing it right off in the lulls.

Centreboard - raise it a little if you are very overpowered. Raking the board back as you rake the mast back can help to maintain balance.

Outhaul - this should now be hard on upwind to keep the lower mainsail flat.

Here the crew has both hands behind his head and is on tiptoes to maximise the righting moment.

on tip-toe with a straight body and one arm behind your head. Use the second arm to trim the jib or throw it behind your head in a big gust. While you are occasionally allowed to 'bounce' your body weight on the trapeze to keep the boat flat it is illegal to do this repeatedly as it is deemed to be 'pumping' (fanning the leech). Note that it can be particularly effective on the tops of waves as it not only keeps the boat flatter, but also helps the helmsman to bear away down the back of the wave.

The rig

It is most important to set up the rig to have the right amount of power. Too much power and the mainsail will be eased too much, stalling the slot and causing drag. Not enough power and you will be underpowered in the lulls with the boat lacking 'bite' and pointing ability. Try to optimise for the lulls and use the cunningham to de-power in the gusts.

VERY WINDY AND SURVIVAL WEATHER

In these conditions everybody will be de-powering the rig and feathering the boat. The crew must be very alert and call the gusts for the helmsman, easing the jib in the big gusts to stop the boat getting blown flat. You will also have to anticipate any difficult boathandling situations as even bearing away behind a starboard tack boat can become a major survival exercise. In twin-trapeze boats the helmsman must try his best to keep the boat flat so it isn't blown over in the gusts or fall in to windward in the lulls and headers. If it's very shifty it's worth the helmsman hooking into the forward toestrap so if you roll to windward slightly he remains locked into the boat and able to sheet in, bear away and get going.

Key Words for
survival weather

ANTICIPATION, BE PHYSICAL, KEEP RACING.

CHECKLIST FOR SURVIVAL WEATHER

Rake - as far back as you can sensibly go without ruining the balance of the boat and making the boom too low for tacking and too near the water, risking a capsize.

Rig tension - you will need lots of rig tension to prevent the jib luff sagging too much and to support the mast.

Spreaders - see medium/strong winds, above

Uppers - see medium/strong winds, above

Diamonds wires - hard on.

Lowers, strut, chocks - let these off to bend the mast low down.

Jib leads - let these right back/up to depower the jib.

Jib luff tension - pull this on hard to depower the jib.

Outhaul - as tight as possible.

Cunningham - as tight as possible, but maybe ease it in any lulls.

Vang (kicking strap) - let this off to open the mainsail leech. Pull it on in the lulls to get some drive.

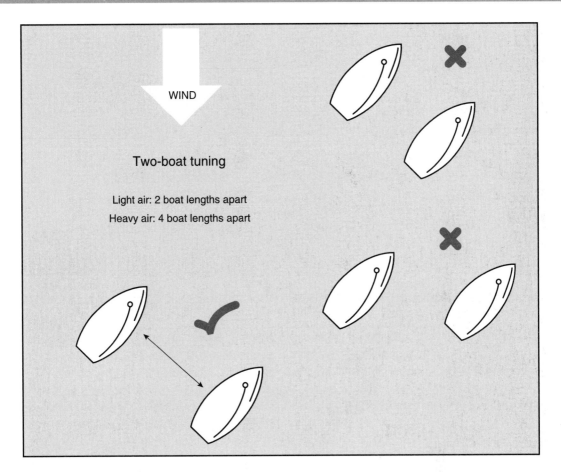

WIND

Two-boat tuning

Light air: 2 boat lengths apart
Heavy air: 4 boat lengths apart

Trim and balance

Keep as far back as necessary to stop the bow
slamming the waves. Keep the boat as flat as
you can by steering accurately and working
hard on the sheets.

TWO-BOAT TUNING

Two- or three-boat tuning is the best way to test
your speed in dinghies, where instrumentation
is of no value. It is by far the best way of
experimenting to find your best settings, which
can then be recorded for future use in racing.
Tuning should be done in the steadiest winds
possible, as shifts and gusts strongly affect the
results. It often takes time to develop an

understanding with a tuning partner and it is
important to find a 'sparring partner' who is
of a similar ability to yourselves and equally
motivated.

- Line up two to four boatlengths apart – too far
  apart and you will be in a different wind, too
  close and you will affect each other's sailing.

- As a guide, line up the windward boat's bow
  with the mast of the leeward boat.

- Make sure only one boat changes settings at
  a time (normally the slower boat as it tries to
  catch up with the faster one).

- Swap from time to time so that a different
  boat is to windward.

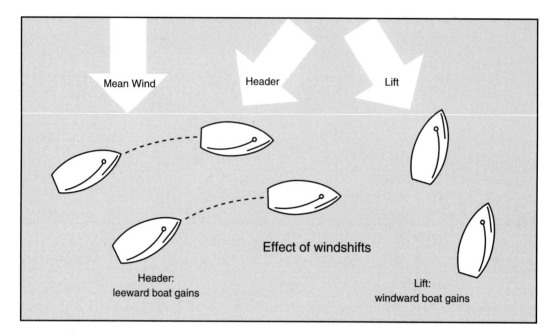

Mean Wind   Header   Lift

Effect of windshifts

Header:
leeward boat gains

Lift:
windward boat gains

- If one boat is consistently faster swap helmsmen and crews to see if it is technique or crew weight that is making the difference and to compare sail shapes.

- Always stop and discuss the results at the end of each run (this can be done downwind to save time).

- You can also tune downwind to test your technique and settings - line up so you don't affect the other boat's wind or waves. Re-start if you get too far apart.

- Watch the compass to monitor the effects of any windshifts (headers will make the leeward boat look faster and vice-versa).

- Be patient - this can be a long process.

DOWNWIND

The downwind legs were once a chance to relax, safe in the knowledge that not too much could be lost in the straight line procession to the leeward mark. This is no longer the case: the dramatic improvements in offwind speed caused by the asymmetric spinnakers and lighter hulls have changed the game beyond recognition. It's fair to say that a new dimension has been added to our sport.

THEORY OF APPARENT WIND

An understanding of apparent wind is now crucial to success at downwind sailing. Catamaran sailors and windsurfers are used to thinking in terms of apparent wind, but for many dinghy and keelboat sailors it is a new concept.

Apparent wind is the actual wind that a boat experiences. It is made up of the true wind component and the component that the boat generates itself, by its own movement. What this means in practice is that your course and speed has a great impact on the wind you experience, which in turn will affect the course you can steer.

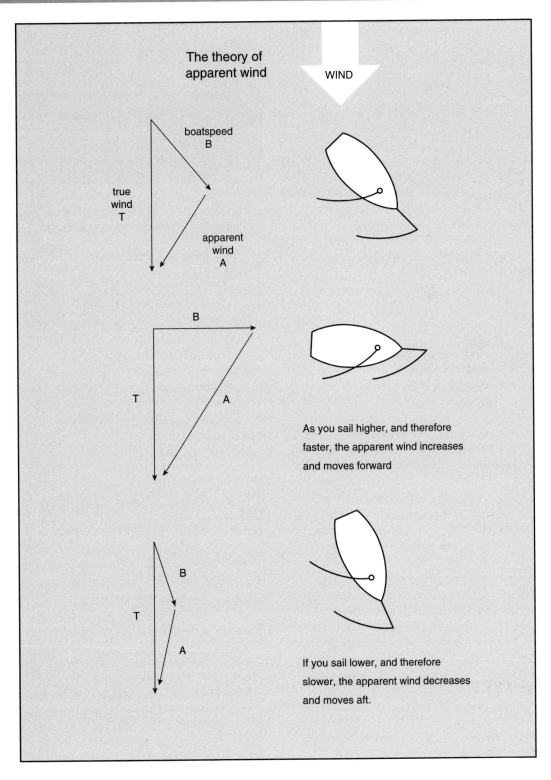

The theory of
apparent wind

WIND

boatspeed
B

true
wind
T

apparent
wind
A

B

T

A

As you sail higher, and therefore
faster, the apparent wind increases
and moves forward

B

T

A

If you sail lower, and therefore
slower, the apparent wind decreases
and moves aft.

Here the spinnaker luff has been eased to power up the asymmetric and help us run low.

Heeling the boat slightly can neutralise the helm, especially when you're trying to sail high and when the mainsail is de-powered.

This is of great interest to us when sailing downwind as the faster we go, the more the apparent wind moves forward and the lower we can then sail.

ASYMMETRIC SPINNAKER TECHNIQUE

With an asymmetric spinnaker we have to sail across the wind, gybing to make our way down to the leeward mark, in much the same way as we sail across the wind and tack to make our way up to the windward mark. Running is, for these boats, a thing of the past. Take care not to collide with other boats – your vision is often impaired and your course less predictable than in a conventional boat.

The art of success with an asymmetric spinnaker is to sail the best VMG (Velocity Made Good). Sail high and you obviously have to sail further, but you will be going faster. Sail low and you will be sailing a more direct route, but will have less boatspeed. Your job is to find the best compromise. The ideal angle is different for every boat and for each set of conditions. You *must* develop a good feel for how high your boat should be sailed to optimise VMG in any given wind and sea state.

Trimming

Trimming an asymmetric is very easy indeed. Simply ease the sheet to keep the luff of the spinnaker curling slightly. The sail won't collapse as quickly as a conventional spinnaker and is therefore very forgiving. The worst mistake is to oversheet the sail. This is most common shortly after gybing, when lots of sheet tension is required to get the spinnaker to the new side and to stop it twisting. (See also 'Laying the gybe mark'.)

Setting up the rig

For running always try to power up the rig up as this will enable you to sail lower. Powering up the mainsail also balances the rig slightly against the extra area provided by the spinnaker.

Power up the rig as follows:

• Ease the cunningham.

• Ease the vang (do this before the windward mark). Be careful not to over-ease as that will let the boom sky and de-power the mainsail.

• Ease the outhaul.

- Do not overtighten the spinnaker luff (ie don't overtighten the halyard).

- Pull the spinnaker tweakers on if needed

- Pull the bowsprit to windward if possible

The centreboard dilemma

Most people tend to leave the centreboard down for four good reasons.

1. The asymmetric spinnaker produces lee helm and the centreboard counteracts this.

2. The centreboard powers up the boat which in turn allows you to steer lower.

3. There is enough to do without worrying about it and you can lose more trying to raise it than leaving it down.

4. You have something to stand on if it all goes horribly wrong!

We recommend, however, that you try to pull it half up as the centreboard has these negative impacts.

1. It causes drag (increases surface area).

2. It generates lift when you want to head low.

3. It makes the boat less forgiving.

Communication

The crew must talk to the helmsman informing him of how much pressure he has on the spinnaker sheet (especially in light airs), to help the helmsman steer a fast course.

Kinetics

With the excitement of an asymmetric spinnaker it's all too easy to forget kinetics. Large gains can be made by pumping, within the rules (which vary from class to class).
Pump both the mainsail and spinnaker together, as this keeps the slot between them constant and has the least effect on the balance of the boat. It can make all the difference when you're trying to plane early or catch waves.

Boat balance and trim

Where possible sail the boat either flat or heeled slightly to leeward. Leeward heel is useful if the boat has a lot of leeward helm because of the spinnaker. The boat's trim should be constantly monitored and changed for any change in conditions. In non-planing weather minimum surface area is a priority and you should sit well forward. In planing conditions the weight should be moved further back until you may be hanging right off the back in survival conditions to prevent nose-diving.

Medium winds/maximum power

These are the easiest conditions to establish the best VMG. In all high-performance boats it should pay to sail quite high initially to get the boat planing, then gradually sail lower as the apparent wind moves forward. If there is any sign of the speed dropping off you will have to head back up slightly to get the boat flying again. In most twin-trapeze boats it will pay to have both of you trapezing downwind, because without the righting moment that the trapezes generate the speed will not increase enough to move the apparent wind right forward. Your course is therefore largely dictated by having to support both of you at full stretch.

In the very light and powerful International 14, which accelerates rapidly when you head up, it nearly always pays to twin-trapeze downwind. In many cases a boat twin-trapezing will actually sail not only faster but lower than a boat that is single-trapezing because of the change in apparent wind. This is the most visible sign of apparent wind theory working in practice.

Light airs

As the wind gradually drops there comes a stage when you have to give up on sailing high and simply sit in and sail lower. This is because in the light breeze you can't increase your speed enough by coming up to affect the apparent wind or compensate for the extra distance you have to sail. This is typically the case as soon as you are displacement sailing. It is still not possible to dead run as the sails won't work efficiently, so the skill is in knowing how low you can sail without slowing the boat too much. The process is quite similar to sailing a conventional spinnaker boat in very light winds, when you have to come up to keep the spinnaker filling. The crew can help the helmsman by indicating when the pressure goes very light in the spinnaker sheet, at which point you must head up to keep it flying. In this wind pulling the centreboard up certainly helps the boat slip off to leeward and reduces drag.

Very windy and survival weather

When it is really blowing getting down the run successfully can be the key to a good result. If there is one secret to success in this weather it is judging how hard to push yourselves and the boat downwind. Generally speaking it pays to fly the spinnaker, as it actually helps to lift the bow and stabilize the boat, but the problem is often getting it up and down. The key is to pick your moment to hoist, gybe and drop, with the helmsman occupying himself solely with keeping the boat upright. Let the crew sort out everything to do with the spinnaker.

When underway with the spinnaker up there may be times when you have to back off and "shelter from the power". Nose-diving is a probability when the hull is at top speed in short

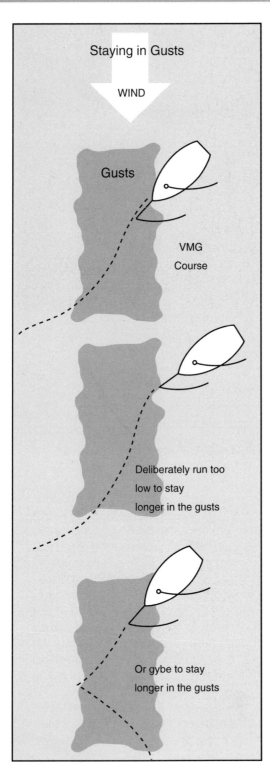

Staying in Gusts

WIND

Gusts

VMG
Course

Deliberately run too
low to stay
longer in the gusts

Or gybe to stay
longer in the gusts

waves, and the best way of avoiding problems is to back off just before they occur (ease the spinnaker sheet or bear away). It is also advisable to keep one eye on the mast as it is under great strain and you may need to pull on some cunningham and even kicking strap to prevent it inverting. Best racing speed is achieved by recognising when problems might occur and backing off for 20% of the time in order to still be there in one piece to race hard for the remaining 80% of the time. Always judge a leg by the wind and waves at the time or by what it's like just to windward, not by how it was last time around. If you are too cautious you will lose and if you are too 'gung ho' you will also lose, no matter how much fun you have in the process!

You can depower the mainsail by leaving the cunningham and outhaul hard on.

In twin wire boats it is often hard for the helmsman to get out on the trapeze and it may be safer to sit in the boat and let the crew trapeze. If possible you should both strap in your feet, with the crew's back leg behind the helmsman's front leg to ensure the weight is as far back as possible.

If the course is fairly long it can even be faster to push hard and capsize once on a run, than sail too slowly all the way down. This is certainly the case if you have good technique for righting the boat and is a good reason to practice. It 's also far more fun hammering downhill!

REACHING WITH THE ASYMMETRIC – LAYING THE GYBE MARK

It is extremely tricky to sail high enough to get round a gybe mark with the asymmetric up in overpowering conditions, but mastering it can save lots of distance that would be lost by

As the boat heels the crew loses righting moment. He should lower himself on the wire to gain angle. Part of the problem is that the vang is too tight.

having to drop the spinnaker. The key tips are:

1. Heel to leeward to get rid of the (considerable) lee helm and spill wind off the top of the rig. Note the boat will slide further sideways, but with less power from the sails and less resistance from the board you will more than compensate for this.

2. Curl as much of the spinnaker's luff as possible to de-power the sail, without collapsing it.

3. Pull the cunningham and outhaul hard on to de-power the mainsail and ease the vang both to de-power the mainsail and keep the boom end out of the water (this would mean

a certain capsize). Be careful not to let the vang off too much if the mast looks like it may invert.

4. Slow the boat by feathering it into the wind and easing the sails so the apparent wind moves aft, which will in turn enable you to head up. Try not to bear off in the gusts as you will only accelerate and sail lower.

5. In trapeze boats it is important that you lower yourself on the trapeze (both helmsman and crew in twin-wire boats). This is because you lose righting moment as you let the boat heel because you are pulled higher on the trapeze.

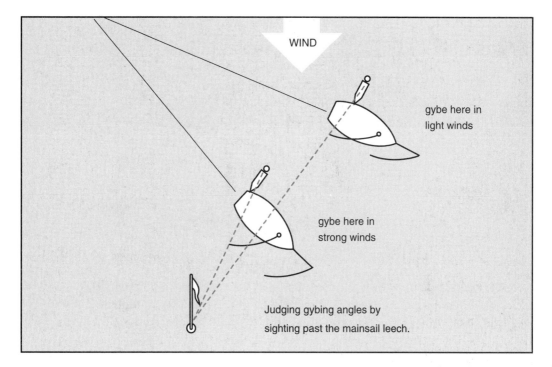

WIND

gybe here in
light winds

gybe here in
strong winds

Judging gybing angles by
sighting past the mainsail leech.

TACTICAL TIPS

The tactics of running with an asymmetric vary considerably from those of conventional spinnaker work.

Staying in the gusts

In conventional spinnaker boats, it's easy to stay in the gusts because you simply bear off and sail directly downwind with the gust for as long as it lasts. With an asymmetric you are sailing across the wind and it's common for you to accelerate in a gust and sail straight out of it. There are two solutions (see diagram on page 81):
a. Gybe just before sailing out of the gust to sail back across it.
b. Sail lower than your best VMG course to sail in the gust for longer. This can be faster than sailing your best VMG, but spending too long in the lulls. Be careful not to run too low and lose the advantages that boatspeed provides in terms of apparent wind.

Judging the laylines

This is not an exact science, as gusts and lulls greatly affect your course. There is no substitute for experience in a particular class to know its gybing angles, but you can make it easier with a few guidelines
a. Always look behind to judge the wind that is coming, as that will dictate your angle.
b. Try to use a reference point on the boat to judge the angle. This can be a mark on the leeward gunwale or a fitting.

Every boat is different, but in many boats the mainsail leech is a good reference point. This works because the windier it is the further back in the boat you move and the earlier you can see the leeward mark around the back of the mainsail leech. This means you gybe earlier which is of course what you want to do when it is windier. In light winds the reverse is true. In catamarans the cross beam is a good reference point as you can sight down it and then make allowances for the tide and wind strength.

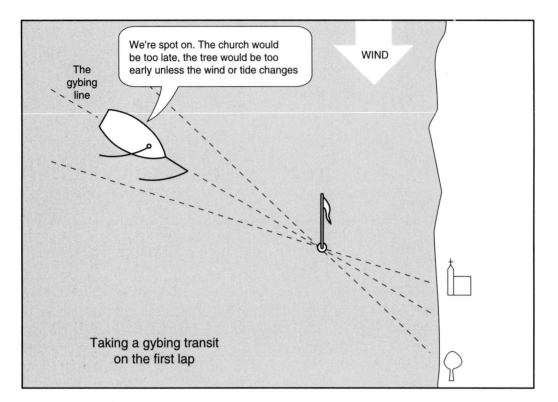

Taking a gybing transit
on the first lap

c. Try to take and remember a transit on the land so that you have a reference point on the next lap, although you must take account of changes in tide and wind direction and pressure.

d. In light winds, if in doubt go a bit further. In strong winds go earlier if in doubt.

What to do if you're not quite getting down to the leeward mark

There is nothing more frustrating than gybing slightly too early and therefore having to run really low or put in two gybes. Try your best to go low by coming up for speed to move the apparent wind forward and then using this to dive low. If you are still not making it, accept that you will need to put in two gybes. Don't be stubborn and lose all your speed by sailing too low for too long.

Judging dirty wind

Asymmetrics have a big windshadow and you must sail in clear air. The windshadow works differently from that in a conventional running boat. The main difference is that you are sailing across the wind and your apparent wind (the wind you use to sail) is therefore coming from further forward than you may think. A boat directly upwind is not actually affecting your wind (see diagram).

Technique summary

Boatspeed both upwind and down comes from attention to detail as it is the sum of all the little parts that makes the boat go fast. If there is one thing that can give you an edge it is spending lots of time in the boat to develop a good sense of feel for how the boat is sailing and therefore what you need to change, if anything, to get going better.

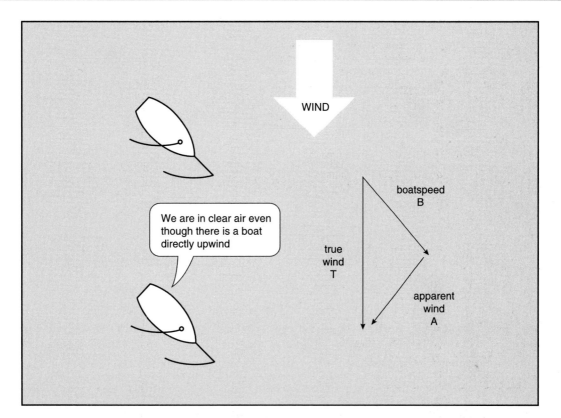

MOST COMMON MISTAKES SAILING DOWNWIND WITH AN ASYMMETRIC

1. Sailing too low and not getting the benefits of apparent wind changes.

2. Forgetting to power up the rig.

3. Sitting too far back in the boat (especially twin-wire boats).

4. Failing to stay in the gusts long enough.

5. Not pumping the sails enough in marginal planing conditions.

6. Misjudging the angles.

7. Sailing in dirty air.

PART FOUR
THE RACING

4   THE RACING

THE OLD 'OLYMPIC COURSE'

The 'triangle, sausage, triangle' as it is popularly known, was devised to best test competitors' abilities on all points of sail, but it is no longer the only option used at championships. This course has been criticised for not being spectator/press friendly enough and was therefore dropped by the ISF for most classes after the 1992 Olympic Games. New courses were developed to try to offer a more exciting form of racing that is less boatspeed orientated, has tighter racing, and which does not take as long to complete.

These new courses – of which the trapezoid and the windward/leeward (Super Cup) course are the best known – are growing rapidly in popularity and have introduced sailors to new tactical situations and new considerations.

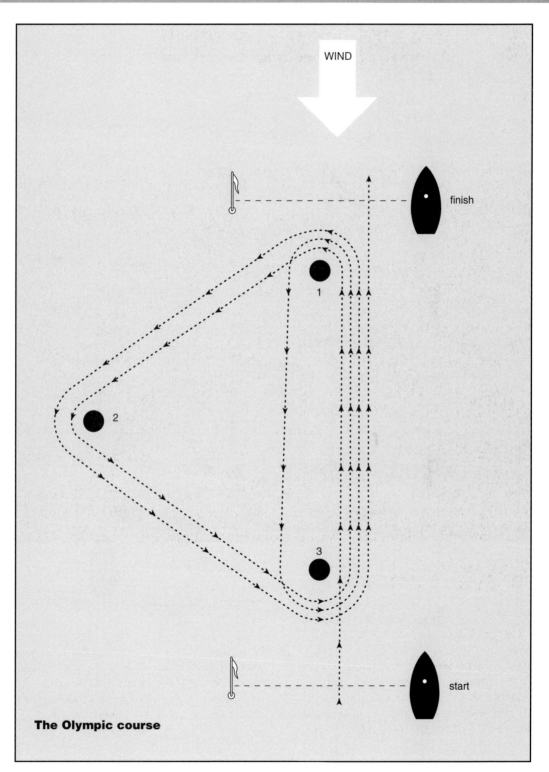

The Olympic course

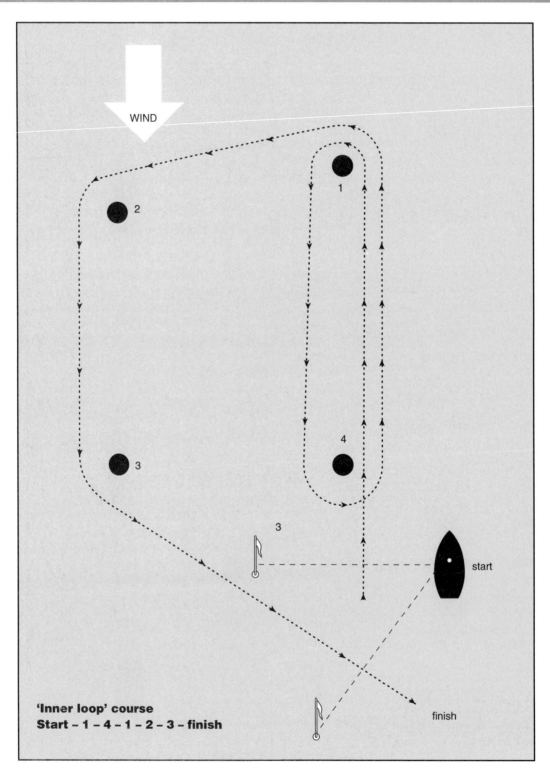

WIND

1

2

3

4

3

start

finish

'Inner loop' course
Start – 1 – 4 – 1 – 2 – 3 – finish

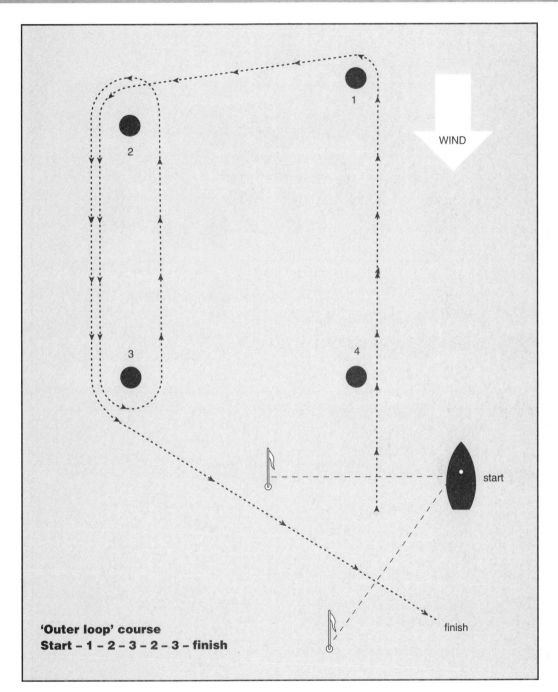

'Outer loop' course
Start – 1 – 2 – 3 – 2 – 3 – finish

THE OLYMPIC TRAPEZOID (INNER AND OUTER LOOP)

The Olympic trapezoid has two variations, the inner and outer loop, which is primarily to allow two fleets to race on the same course at the same time with little chance of ever meeting

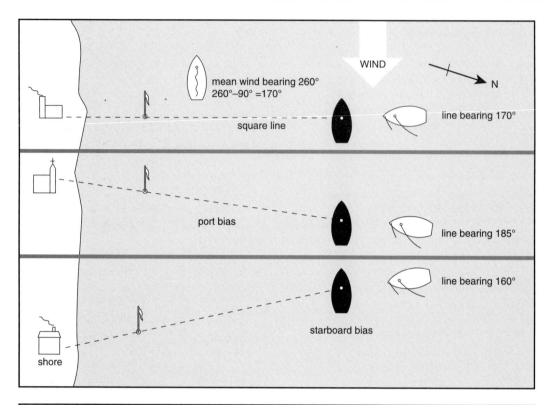

mean wind bearing 260°
260°–90° =170°

WIND

N

square line

line bearing 170°

port bias

line bearing 185°

line bearing 160°

starboard bias

shore

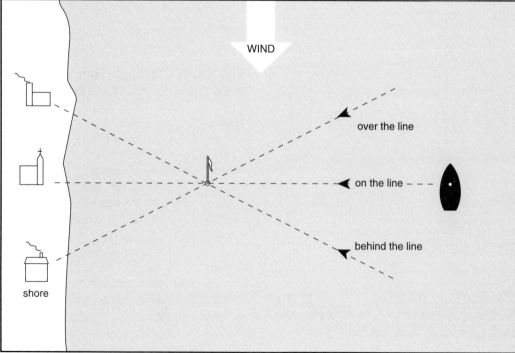

WIND

over the line

on the line

behind the line

shore

each other. The length of the course legs should be set to make the races last about 45 to 60 minutes and this means that the legs are much shorter than on a triangle, sausage course which can last 2 to 3 hours. This in turn means that these courses become very congested when there are over 40 one-design boats.

Pre-start

It is common to now have only 3 minutes between starting signals with the whole sequence only lasting 6 minutes. This means that time is short and you have to be very organised in order to be well prepared for the actual start. You should aim to be at the starting area at least 30 minutes before the start to have time to carry out the following tasks.

1. Set up the rig and get used to the prevailing conditions.

2. Find the course marks, plan the first beat and look at the reaches.

3. Check the start line bias.

4. Find and remember start line transits (check after preparatory signal).

5. Check the spinnaker for twists etc.

6. Monitor the wind and get compass bearings for upwind work.

7. Check for weed and keep the cockpit dry.

THE START

With shorter start lines on the new courses, start line bias is less important than it used to be. The main priority is to start on the line with good speed and in clear air: this very often means conceding some line bias to gain space on the line. With the shorter upwind legs it is also more important than ever to plan your start around your upwind gameplan.

Starting options when wanting to go right up the first beat

Option A. (Diagram page 94.) It will require good boathandling but starting at the starboard end will give you the best opportunity to tack onto port and go right.

Option B. Approach on port tack behind the fleet until the gun. Good acceleration is then needed to squirt through a gap, putting you into clear air and to the right of the competition. (A high risk/high reward manoeuvre, beware Rule 36.)

Option C. The conservative option is to start one third down from the starboard end, tacking onto port at the nearest available clear air lane.

Starting options when wanting to go left up the first beat

Option A. (Diagram page 95.) The perfect pin end start, requiring controlled aggression and confidence in your boathandling.

Option B. Tack from port to starboard into a gap in the last 40 seconds, while making a nice space to leeward to accelerate into at the gun.

Option C. Start a third of the way from the pin to avoid getting caught in the chaos. This is the conservative and often preferred option.

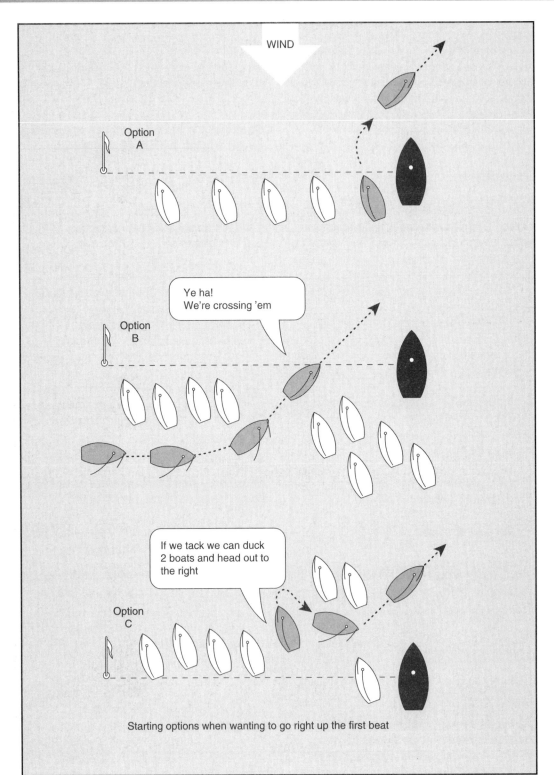

Starting options when wanting to go right up the first beat

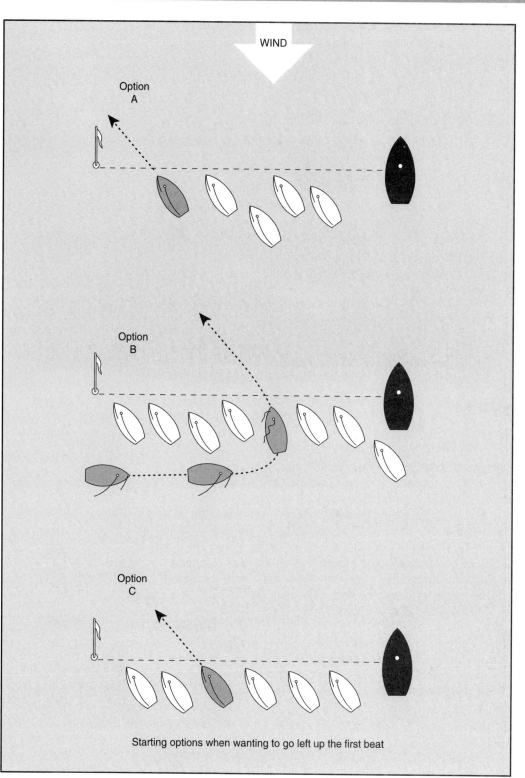

WIND

Option
A

Option
B

Option
C

Starting options when wanting to go left up the first beat

The conservative option would be to start one-third of the way down the line!

Starting mid-line

When the wind is oscillating and showing no particular favoured side, working the middle of the beat is going to be your best route upwind. You must be able to get in phase with the oscillations as soon as possible after the start.

A mid-line start will give you the best chance to make maximum use of the windshifts, providing you can get a good transit and start in the front row. (Beware of line sag and bulge.)

Always have a plan for the start and be determined to carry it out. But if the start is going wrong and you are getting boxed in, don't be afraid to bail out and either approach the line with speed on port or start elsewhere on starboard.

The key to a good start remain the same as always!

1. Space to leeward to accelerate into.

2. Being in the front rank (covered by others if you might be over).

3. Timing your final approach to hit the line with speed.

Problems of fully-battened sails

Most high-performance boats now have fully-battened sails and these tend to hold the boat head to wind, so take special care not to get stuck in irons. Having no vang tension will help you bear off and will also help you to accelerate just before the gun.

Note the bulges and sags at this start.
A transit enables the boats in a sag to start well clear of their neighbours.

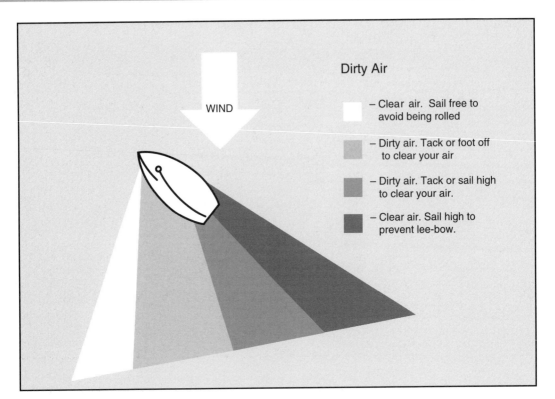

Dirty Air

— Clear air. Sail free to avoid being rolled

— Dirty air. Tack or foot off to clear your air

— Dirty air. Tack or sail high to clear your air.

— Clear air. Sail high to prevent lee-bow.

FIRST BEAT

Clear air after the start

The number one priority must be to sail in as much clear air as possible. If you sail in dirty air you will not be in the top few at the windward mark. If you have had a bad start this will mean tacking off soon after the start if you are unable to find clear air on starboard. The crew can play an important role here by telling the helmsman of any opportunities to tack, even if it will mean having to duck and pass behind starboard tack boats.

Keeping a clear air lane

Once you have cleared the starting area it is crucial to start heading the way you think will pay, in a 'lane' of clear air. This means timing any tacks in such a way that there is little chance of anybody tacking on you. Tacking in high-performance boats costs distance even if you are very well drilled, and you can ill-afford to tack only to be forced back the wrong way again soon afterwards. The sooner you can settle down in a lane of clear air, the sooner you can settle into a rhythm and start to think about windshifts and tactics.

Cross them while you can

How often have we heard tales of people who 'could have crossed the fleet' but who ended up being 'really unlucky'. The lesson to be learned is that if you have had a good start and are able to cross the fleet, then why not do it? You don't have to sail all the way across, but at least cross the main bunch before tacking back, thereby securing a good position at the windward mark.

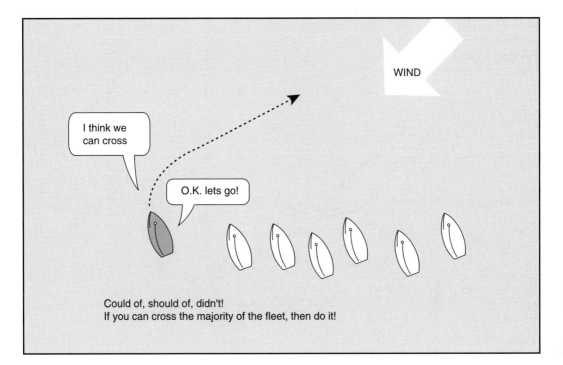

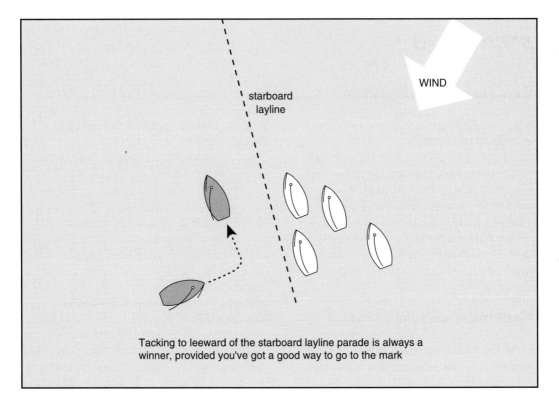

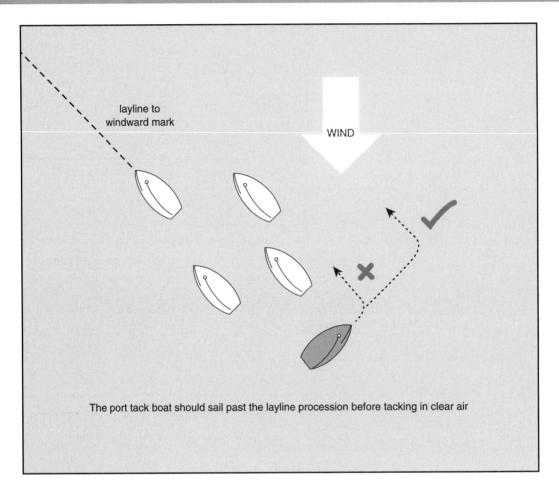

layline to
windward mark

WIND

The port tack boat should sail past the layline procession before tacking in clear air

Approaching the windward mark

No sooner have you settled down on the first beat, than it is time to start thinking about your approach to the windward mark. If you are leading then you can approach the mark how you like and you will have clear air. But if you're not, then you must judge the spread of all the boats ahead of you and how they are likely to approach the windward mark, so that you can avoid them and stay in clear air for as long as possible without overstanding the mark. As a general rule, any distance that you can make back towards the centre of the course in clear air when in a mid-fleet position, is distance well worth taking.

Avoid the starboard layline if possible

The layline is the one place that you can guarantee will be congested, and clear air is only possible by overstanding. Try to avoid exposing yourself to the threat of the layline by getting back towards the centre of the beat a couple of hundred yards earlier.

What if you do end up near the layline?

In a high-performance boat it usually pays to go slightly further, as another couple of boatlengths can provide an approach in clear air and

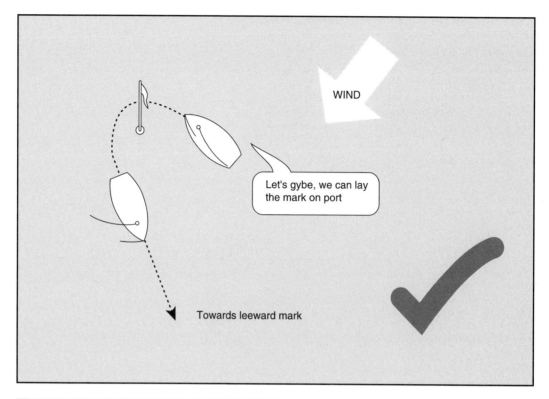

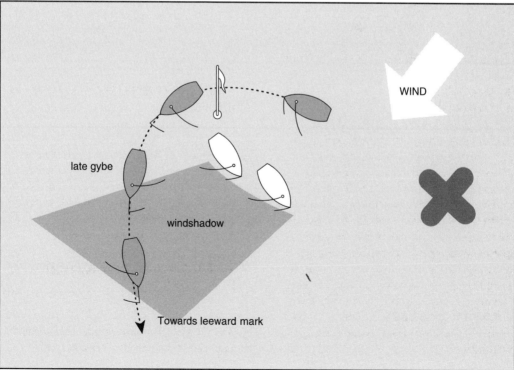

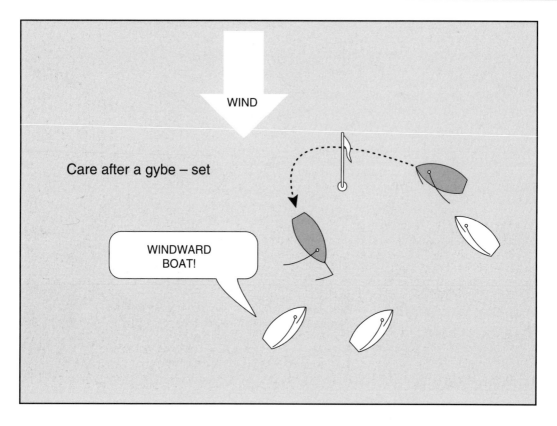

smooth water and that can mean you roll over many boats bogged down on or near the layline. This is especially true in boats that foot fast (ie not hiking boats or keelboats).

INNER LOOP (FIRST RUN)

You should plan your first run before the windward mark so that you know whether you are likely to gybe set or straight set. This is important as you can then prepare the hoist. It also affects whether you need to round the windward mark on the inside or not.

When to gybe set

1. When the run is skewed so that most of the run will be sailed on port tack. Note that if you gybe too late you will find yourself in dirty air for the rest of the run.

2. When there is a major temporary shift to the right (ie a veer) that would give you the best initial angle on port tack.

3. When there is considerably more wind or less tide on the left of the run.

4. When you think a clear-air advantage can be gained as most people are straight setting.

The dangers of doing a gybe set

1. It is slower than a straight set.

2. You have to sail underneath any boats still approaching the windward mark on the

starboard layline. This hurts, especially in light winds but is not too bad in a breeze when the waves carry you down lower on the hoist and you sail a lower angle away from them.

3. You must be very careful not to infringe boats still approaching the windward mark.

> IF IN ANY DOUBT DO A
> STRAIGHT SET, AS IT'S LESS
> OF A GAMBLE.

Once you are away from the windward mark you can start to settle down and concentrate on your boatspeed and tactics.

Clear air

This is still incredibly important and you should always aim to keep your air clear as much as possible. This means keeping a wary eye on what is happening behind. Generally speaking packs of boats go slowly and you should make every effort to get clear wind and water away from nearby boats. To do this consider gybing, sailing too high or too low in order to gain space, when you can resume your VMG course. Although you lose slightly initially, this space can make you sail the whole run faster.

Pressure (wind strength)

Staying in the strongest wind is very important and the helmsman must keep a constant vigil to spot the gusts as they move down the course.

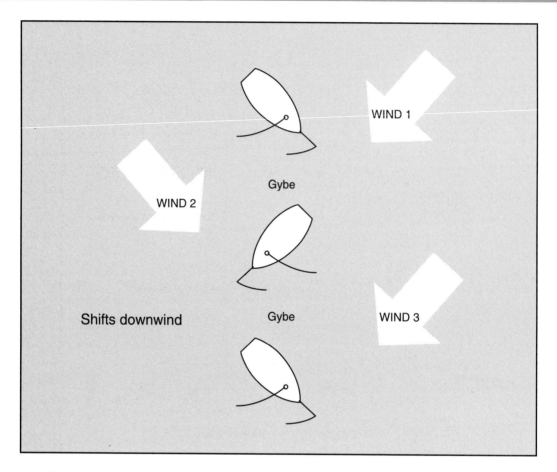

Windshifts

These are as important downwind as upwind and you should watch boats behind to get clues on approaching shifts.

Try to gybe on the lifts and sail down the headers. Having a good gybing technique will encourage you to gybe more for tactical gain.

Approaching the leeward mark

You should plan this when half-way down the run. Try to work out how the fleet is spread and how they are likely to approach the leeward mark. Try to avoid the laylines to the mark as you will then be gybed on by boats behind and be left with no option but to sail slowly in dirty

air. If it is very congested try to make your way to the inside and consider approaching the leeward mark on starboard, as you will then have water on everybody.

THE LEEWARD MARK

The drop

If you are sailing the inner loop course your next downwind leg is a tight reach and having the spinnaker in the port bag will make for an easier hoist. You therefore need to do a straight drop if you're on port tack and a gybe drop or float drop if you're on starboard (A float drop is a conventional spinnaker drop where the pole is

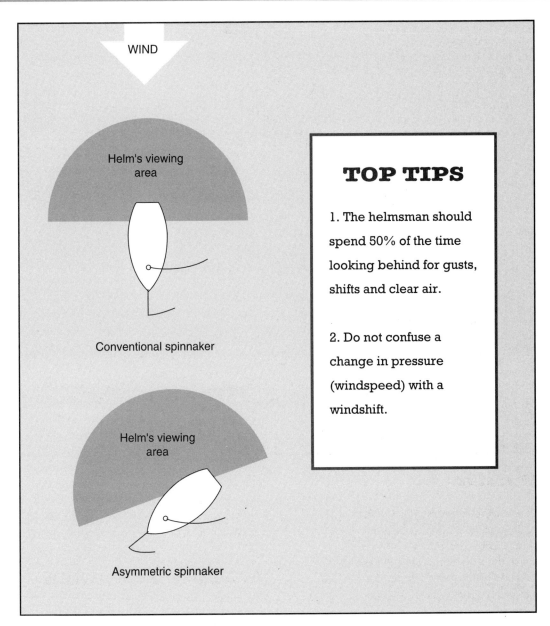

WIND

Helm's viewing area

Conventional spinnaker

Helm's viewing area

Asymmetric spinnaker

TOP TIPS

1. The helmsman should spend 50% of the time looking behind for gusts, shifts and clear air.

2. Do not confuse a change in pressure (windspeed) with a windshift.

removed, before gybing and then dropping the spinnaker.) If things get very hectic it may be more important tactically to do the easiest possible drop at the time in order to get round in good shape and worry about the hoist when you get there.

The rounding

A good leeward mark rounding can not only save many places, but can dictate the first part of the second beat. Make every effort to get water and round on the inside in relatively clear air. If there are boats inside you or a pile-up ahead try to slow down and let them clear so

that you can round neatly, as opposed to driving on to leeward of the mess.

When does it pay to go around the outside?

1. When you want to go right on the beat and it is worth footing under people to the right.

2. When your momentum can actually carry you around and into clear air quickly (i.e. very light airs).

3. If there is a big raft, avoid it by simply sailing around it.

THE SECOND BEAT

The second beat should be easier than the first as you now have more information (that you learned on the first beat) and there should be more space in which to settle down and sail to the windshifts. The beat is relatively short and any time on the wrong tack will prove costly. This means that as soon as possible after the leeward mark rounding you must compare your compass heading to your pre-start and first beat numbers. If you are on a header and you think the wind will shift back later, then you must tack. If you are lifted then carry on (sometimes this is more important than getting clear air).

The second beat for the leaders will probably be a time of consolidation, while they also concentrate on fighting for the major honours. They don't need to take unnecessary risks. For those in the middle there is everything to play for and you must decide whether to consolidate or gamble. Risks can be punished hard! For the tail-enders it may well be time to start to take some tactical risks to get back into the pack. You must remember, however, that there is no point in banging a corner for the sake of it. The best way to catch up is to sail the fastest route, and

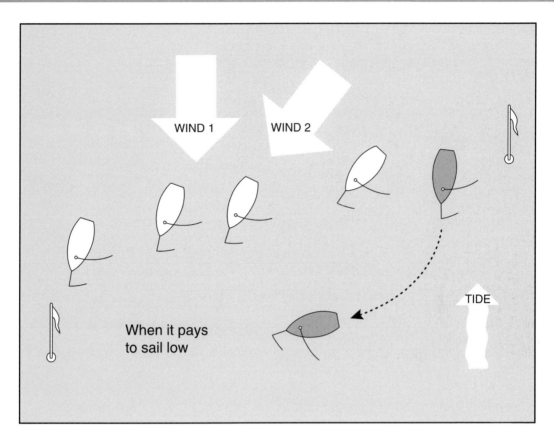

WIND 1   WIND 2

TIDE

When it pays
to sail low

that may well be up the middle. It's amazing how many boats it is possible to overtake by sailing the right way with good speed. Try not to panic!

TOP REACH

Before getting to the top mark you must find mark 2 and try to judge how tight the reach will be. If the crew can spot a reference point on distant land that will give the helmsman something to aim for as he bears away at the top mark. The biggest danger on the top reach is going slightly low and being rolled by many boats. Therefore the standard tactic is to protect your wind by staying in the high lane and trying to pick off those boats that fail to do so or make bad hoists.

The fleet always tends to sail too high as they fight for clear air and luff each other. Going low is very tempting and can pay, but this is far less common than it used to be on the old courses as the leg is shorter and normally laid tighter to the wind. Going low will mean getting dirty air as you leave the windward mark and as you approach the gybe mark. It will however mean sailing a more direct route and being inside at mark 2. (This is less important than on the old triangle courses as the next leg is a run, not a reach.)

> **IF IN DOUBT STAY HIGH**
> **WHEN THERE ARE LOTS OF**
> **BOATS AROUND**

TOP TIPS FOR THE REACH

1. Do not pull up the spinnaker until you are confident you will not be rolled by any boats directly behind (wait till they bear off and go for their hoist), and until you are confident that you can lay the next mark with it up (especially if it's windy).

2. If you are going to sail low, do so directly at the windward mark to get separated from the 'high lane' as quickly and by as far as possible.

3. Try not to get involved in luffing battles as this lets the leaders get away. Encourage boats behind not to try and sail over you, and do not try to roll over those in front unless you are fairly certain they will not get up and stop you before you are over them.

4. If you can't find the next mark stay high and sail without the spinnaker if it is windy, but it is probably safe to hoist in light winds.

5. Try to spot mark 2 and judge its angle when you round the windward mark for the first time so you are prepared the second time around.

When can it pay to sail low?

1. When the reach is very broad, normally due to a right hand windshift (veer) or lots of tide flowing upwind.

2. When there is a pack of boats in front that will go very high, but few boats just behind to sail over you.

3. When you think the wind will go right and broaden the leg. This will make it hard for the boats that are high to get down.

4. When you are at the back of the fleet and have nobody left to roll you!

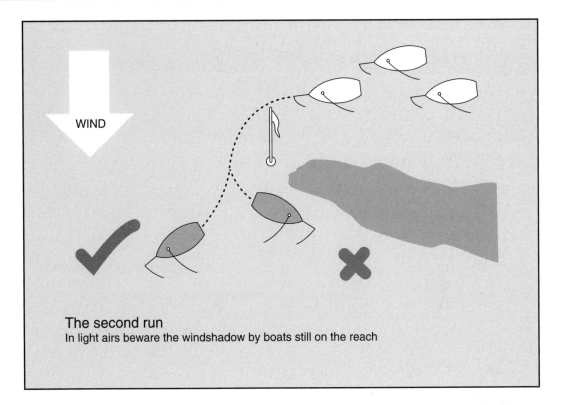

The second run
In light airs beware the windshadow by boats still on the reach

To fly or not to fly on a tight reach

Often it will be unclear whether or not it will pay to fly the spinnaker. Consider the following points

1. If you are nearly fully-powered without the spinnaker, then you will be overpowered with it up and this may be slower.

2. You will lose distance and height hoisting it on a tight reach.

3. You will lose even more if you have to drop it to lay the gybe mark.

4. If you can hoist it and make it pay you will gain as others hoist at mark 2.

5. Asymmetrics can be made to sail very high in light winds.

6. Your race situation can help you decide. If you are in a good position then cover what the opposition do. If you are desperate it may be worth doing something different.

7. Try to decide early on as you then know whether to try to sail straight for mark 2 (up and down in the lulls and gusts), or to stay high and maybe hoist halfway along the leg.

SECOND RUN

This run is essentially the same as the first run except that you are punished less by gybing at the top as there are no boats coming upwind on the starboard layline. Be careful in light winds, however, as there is a windshadow effect from the reaching boats behind, and if you are sailing higher angles you will be quite near these boats.

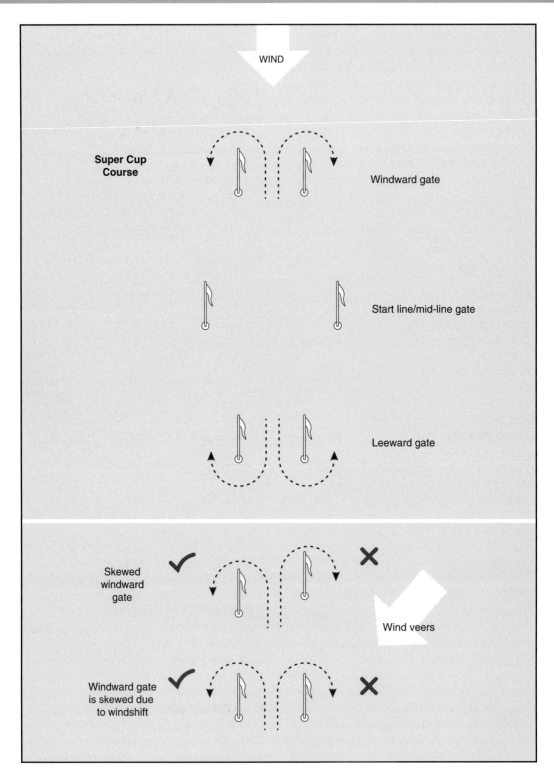

WIND

Super Cup Course

Windward gate

Start line/mid-line gate

Leeward gate

Skewed windward gate

Wind veers

Windward gate is skewed due to windshift

If you are in a bad position this is perhaps your last chance to make a big gain by taking a tactical risk. Essentially this means splitting away from the bulk of the fleet just ahead and praying that you get either a gust or a favourable shift to come back in on (stranger things have been known).

Last leeward mark

It is crucial to be on the inside here as you are then in the high lane for the last tight reach. Do not round outside people. It is better to slow down and go behind them to keep your wind clear. Be careful of gybing right at the leeward mark onto port as it can allow others coming in on port to head up inside you as you sort yourself out from the gybe. It is far better to try to gybe early leaving at least 1-2 boatlengths on port before the mark so that you can do a neat rounding. This is especially true in conventional spinnaker boats as the pole can take a while to gybe.

LAST REACH

This reach is essentially the same as the top reach. The main decision will be whether you can fly the spinnaker or not. This decision should be made as you approach the leeward mark. Consider all the factors outlined above, but bear in mind that it is already up so if in doubt keep it up! You will lose less by dropping it halfway along the reach than by dropping it and then finding that you do need it. If you are unsure and decide to drop, always try to drop it in the starboard bag so that you can do a fast hoist.

The last reach can be very processional but do not give up trying as every place counts. One lapse in concentration such as letting the spinnaker collapse can be enough to get rolled and lose places. As you settle on the reach try to judge the angle of the finishing

line as there can be enough bias to enable you to take a place by heading for the right end.

THE WINDWARD/ LEEWARD (SUPER CUP) COURSE

There is little difference between these courses and the first 2 legs of an inner loop trapezoid course. The main differences are that the legs are often even shorter so that you do more rounds, and the first beat can be very short if the start is in the middle of the beat. In this case it is worth bearing in mind that the starboard end of the startline controls the fleet and you may not be able to tack soon enough and cross from the port end. In this situation it is imperative to try and start at the starboard end so that you are free to tack onto port at the port layline.

The second best start is often the boat that first ducks the fleet on port, but which can then tack back further up the beat onto the controlling starboard tack.

GATES

Turning marks often cause pile-ups and always lead to the fleet spreading out. Gates are increasingly being used in their place. You may find a windward mark gate, a mid-line gate (this often doubles as the start line) and a leeward gate. These gates demand a different tactical approach and can lead to new passing opportunities.

Windward mark gate

The first and main priority here is bias. Is either end of the gate downwind of the other? If so it

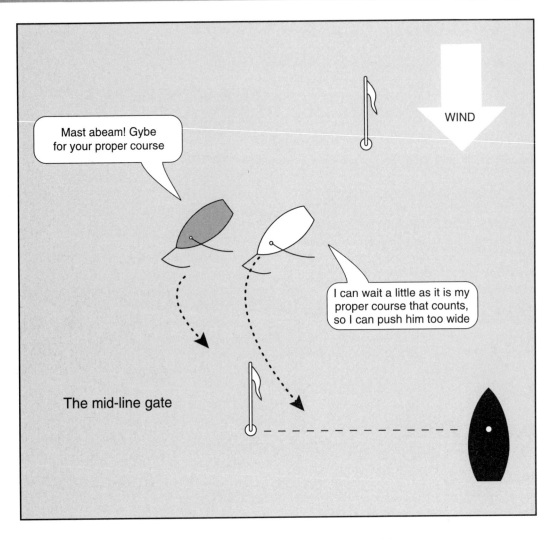

is obviously not only nearer when heading upwind, but also already further downwind for the next leg, giving a double benefit.

If the gate is biased

Head for the favoured end unless it is too congested or there is such a strong tactical reason for going to the other one that it could end up paying to go there and sail the slightly longer course faster.

NB In shifty winds it will pay to have an open mind and not commit yourself, as one windshift could change the bias.

If the gate is square (no bias)

In this case the main priority is which buoy you can get to faster in terms of sailing the best shifts, doing the least tacks and sailing in the clearest wind. The right-hand buoy may well be hard to get to when approaching on port as there could be many right-of-way starboard tackers. Another concern is your likely tactics for the run. If you want to go right on the run for a tactical reason (tide, wind, skewed course

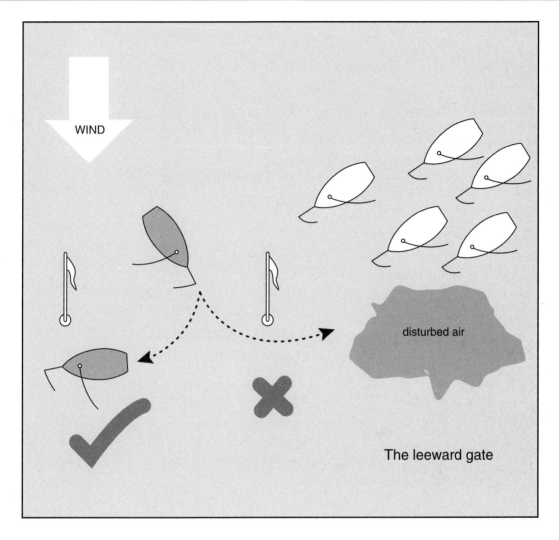

WIND

disturbed air

The leeward gate

etc), then it will make sense to go around the left-hand gate marker and vice-versa. The simplest factor and the best to stick to if in doubt is to go round the mark that has the least boats heading for it and which will therefore give the best chance of clear air.

Mid-line gate downwind

This gate is not a problem if it is large, and you should simply build it into your offwind strategy. Bias is not important as you are simply passing through it. If the gate is small, however, it may

be worth planning to come through on starboard when there are other boats close by. This approach has the added advantage of leaving you just one gybe to complete to round a leeward mark to port (assuming you gybe in the right place). When it is windy, don't leave yourself too tight an angle to get through the gate as one gust can lead to disaster. This is most common when you have been held on by a boat to leeward (especially on starboard). Remember that if you have mast abeam the leeward boat must not sail above *its proper course*, which includes gybing when it needs to go through the gate. Your best strategy is either to shout at the leeward boat to make it gybe as early as possible, or to sail high, slow down and gybe behind it.

The leeward gate

This is essentially the same as the windward gate in that you must consider the bias of the gate and try to head for the buoy that is most upwind. There are three more main considerations at a leeward mark gate.

1. What is going to be the easiest approach from your current position (both for boathandling and boatspeed)?

2. Which way do you want to go on the next beat?

3. Which buoy will be least congested?

Mid-line gate upwind

Like the downwind gate the bias is not important if you simply have to pass through it. Tactically the main thing to avoid is getting on one of the laylines to the gate and suffering from dirty wind.

The finish line

The finish will normally be at the mid-line gate and can be upwind or down. The main consideration is line bias – ie which end is nearer. This must then be weighed against which part of the line is easiest to get to (least tacks or gybes and clearest air). If you are in a close finish it is well worth turning to cross the line at right angles (shortest route) for the last boatlength, using your momentum to get you to the line as quickly as possible.

SUMMARY

Super Cup courses are tight and exciting, with gates adding new tactical considerations. Teams that communicate well, anticipate other boats' actions and keep in clear air and out of trouble will be rewarded with good finishing positions.

Perhaps more than ever the crew has an important role to play in feeding the helmsman all relevant information so that both can plan ahead and make good snap decisions when required.

Risk management....

Rules

While gates cause less congestion than solitary marks, they do produce more crossing incidents as boats pass through the gates. You need to keep your eyes open, anticipate other boats' actions and be careful not to infringe any rules.

CHAMPIONSHIP STRATEGY

Risk management

Sailing is a game of controlled risk taking. Risks can often provide handsome rewards, but can also court disaster. Choosing when to take risks and when to sail safely can determine your level of success. With a longer series of shorter races it is often wise to be conservative to begin with and build a platform of good results which can give you more confidence to take risks later in the series. In a short series with fewer boats, the winning boat will probably have few points and steady good results will not be good enough to win.

Minimise your mistakes

Teams that are successful in sailing are often built up to be superhuman individuals that can 'read the wind' etc., but the reality is actually much simpler. The teams that win are the teams that make fewer mistakes than their opponents. Sailing is a very complicated mistake-making game. In a competitive fleet with a long series it is often not the number of firsts that decides the winner, but in fact the least number of poor results.

Play to strengths & minimise weaknesses

Every team has strengths and weaknesses and understanding these can not only help in your training, but can help you with a strategy. For example, if you have good speed but are not confident in your starting then try to concede some line bias to start in clear air and use your boatspeed. If the opposite is true then it is probably worth mixing it on the start to get the best start to ensure a good weather mark rounding.

Never give up

If ever there was a sport where it pays to keep trying then it is sailing. The race is never over until you have crossed the finish line and until then anything can happen. Sailing history is full of examples of people "snatching defeat from the jaws of victory" and vice-versa. The same is true of championship series, which can show remarkable changes in fortune. Even if the first few races have not gone to plan, there is often still time to turn things around.

SUMMARY

In order to achieve your goal in any given regatta it is important to have a strategy, as this will affect your sailing style. This strategy should be governed by the nature and format of the regatta and revised as the series progresses.

PART FIVE
PLANNING
TO SUCCEED

5 PLANNING TO SUCCEED

Whether you are ambitious in your sailing or simply sail and race for the thrill of it, your enjoyment will be enhanced by the satisfaction of setting and achieving goals within the sport. In addition your performance will improve by following this goal setting approach.

Goal setting is the foundation upon which all our sailing campaigns are based.

WHAT IS A GOAL?

Goals are personal things that essentially represent what you wish to achieve. It could be your life dream such as 'to win the America's Cup' or any personal ambition such as to finish in the top 20 at your national championship. To plan how to go about achieving your goal, the next stage is to break it down into smaller, more tangible goals. An example is to get consistent, good starts. This smaller goal can then be broken down even further into tiny goals such as always to get on the water 20 minutes before the start and form a pre-start plan, or always to be on time and in the front rank on the start. By following this process it is possible to end up with a list of small-scale feasible goals which you can work on and which can affect the larger scale goal that you started out with. Goal setting is in itself a skill, because if you set yourself bad goals you will end up concentrating on the wrong things or with the wrong emphasis in your training or racing.

What is a good/bad goal?

Good goals have a number of qualities which are summed up by the initials SMART.

S stands for specific. The clearer the goal, the easier it is to see a way to achieve it.

M stands for measurable. I you are able to gain confidence from reaching your goal, you need to be able to know that you have achieved it.

A is related to achievable. Goals which are too difficult get ditched; but goals which are too easy go the same way. They need to be challenging if you are to think them worthwhile, and get maximum benefit from them.

R means relevant. It is all to easy to work on your good points, but effective goal-setting demands that you work on your weaknesses.

T is time-phased. You need to think of goals over short, medium and long terms. Finally, goals need to be positive. 'Don't capsize' is an example of a negative goal. What was the first thing that came into your head as you read it? 'Keep the boat upright' carries a much more positive image, and one which would be better to adhere to!

A bad goal is a goal that does not fit the above model.

EXAMPLE OF SETTING AND ACHIEVING A GOAL

Aim:

To finish in the top 10 at your fleet nationals in the summer.

Weakness:

Spinnaker hoists and drops (scored 4/10, needs to be 7/10).

Goals:

To analyse the best in your class by April.

To practise 5 hoists/drops every time you go afloat.

To get somebody to watch/video you and analyse your technique.

Eliminating your weaknesses

One way in which goal setting can be used is to eliminate your current weaknesses. To work out what they are, list the key areas that are important to sailing performance and then score yourselves from 1 to 10. Secondly work out how high you need to score in order to achieve your main sailing objective or 'goal', and then work out which areas you most fall short in. You do not need to score yourself 10 out of 10 in all areas to achieve your goal.

(For instance, when scoring yourself on rules knowledge you may need to be at level 9 or 10 to win the team racing or match racing world championship, but you could probably win a fleet racing nationals with only a 6 or 7 out of 10.)

Once you have established your weaknesses then set yourself some SMART goals which will help improve your performance in those areas.

Goals summary

Goals are very powerful tools that can help you target your racing and training. It is a good idea to set yourself just a few SMART goals every time you go afloat as well as those over longer timescales. Monitor your progress and be critical as to whether you have fulfilled your goals or not. Goals, and indeed the whole mental side of the game, are very well covered in *Mental & Physical Fitness for Sailing* (see page 128).

THE TEAM

Few high-performance boats are single-handers and you will therefore need to work well as a team. Choosing who to sail with is perhaps the single most important decision you will face in your campaign. Many partnerships do not flourish and some end in acrimony. Having a good crew is becoming more and more important in high-performance boats in particular and especially over the new shorter courses. A good team will nearly always beat a boat containing two individuals.

Choosing your partner

In the case of a two-person dinghy a

successful partnership should have the following ingredients:

- A mutually-shared goal. (It won't work if one of you wants to win the worlds while one of you prefers golf, but wants to sail because of the social life.)

- Correct physical size / weight for the boat.

- A sense of fun – you will need to be able to have a laugh if things go wrong as they will almost certainly do at some time.

- A mix of talents. You don't need two rules, organisational, weather, technical or tactical experts, but one of you should have a good feel for each area.

- An agreed policy on financial and time commitments.

- An ability to communicate with each other openly. Bottling up feelings leads to future explosions!

- A mutual trust in each others abilities (are you really a team if you don't trust your partner's abilities or judgement?).

Even if you have all the above ingredients, teamwork has to be worked on and tends to develop over time. Never underestimate the contribution that your partner is making and make sure he knows that you are grateful. Divide the tasks – it can work very well if you trust each other to take care of different areas of a campaign, preparation or the race. An

example would be that one of the team does most of the boatwork, while the other sorts out travel and accommodation arrangements. At a regatta a good example is one person sorting out the tides and the weather while the other sorts out the lunch!

A well known and successful J24 crew had a system for all major championships. The helmsman checked the sailing instructions and notice board, the trimmer sorted out an up-to-date weather forecast and tidal information, the pit man checked the standing and running rigging and set it for the day's perceived conditions, the bowman organised the boat down below (water, sails, safety regs etc) and the 5th person sorted out all the food and drink for the day.

TIME AND MONEY MANAGEMENT

Most unsuccessful sailing campaigns fail as a direct result of lack of money or lack of time. Not all successful sailing campaigns, however, have had the most time or money. The key here is in the management of what you have.

Money

Money is always a problem and you will have to prioritise what money you do have. No matter how scary it can become it's a good idea to budget your campaign carefully so that you don't end up running out of money just before your main event. Sponsorship is growing within our sport and may now be allowed within your class rules, but sponsors are not easy to find and often demand a large time input. The best advice with any sponsor is to do your best to keep them happy as it is · often said that they are easier to keep than to get in the first place!

SUMMARY

Good planning can help to achieve the following:

- Best use of available time.

- Best use of available money/resources.

- Best teamwork.

- Steepest learning curve.

- Best chance of achieving of your goal.

Time

All sailing campaigns run out of time and in the case of both the Whitbread Round the World Race and the America's Cup it is very often those syndicates with most time on the water that end up being successful. Prioritising your time is essential, as is not wasting it. You may not have enough leisure hours in the week to work on the boat, do some physical training, look for sponsors, race and train, so what is going to give? When sailing, you may not have enough time to do all the racing, boathandling practice and boatspeed work you would like, so what will have to go?

One exercise that helps to focus the mind is to count how many sailing days there are,

Sponsorship is a two-way process. They have to feel they're getting value for money.

allowing for lost days due to weather, before your target regatta. Hopefully, with good goal setting you should be able to prioritise your time better.

Equipment

For those sailing strict one-designs there are few equipment choices to be made. For more open classes, equipment decisions are crucial. The best advice we can give is always to start in a class by buying a good second-hand boat that is well set up and in no way extreme. Try to buy the hull, mast, sails and foils that are currently doing well in the fleet. If you want to try something new, wait until you have more experience in the class.

- 'Standard kit' is undoubtedly the best starting point.

- Be careful of ever trying anything new at a target regatta.

- If you are ever really fast try to preserve that equipment.

At some stage it may be tempting to try to optimise according to predicted conditions at your target regatta. This kind of 'gamble' has been known to pay off, but more often you will find the locals telling you at the regatta, "It's not normally like this"!

In 1988 Mike McIntyre and Bryn Vaile won the Gold Medal in the Star Class in Pusan. Knowing

*that the winds in Pusan were likely to be strong
and that they could measure in 2 sails, they
decided to take a mainsail made out of heavier
sailcloth for very windy days. They had to win
the last race and used this sail, and were
successful. Although there were many reasons
for their success, their willingness to optimise
their equipment played a major role that year.*

LEARNING

How are you going to learn and improve? In
tennis or swimming, the answer might to be to
enlist the help of a coach, but in sailing this is
rarely the case. Coaches do have a role to
play and club coaching sessions are very
valuable. Unfortunately they are all too rarely
available and the answers must often come
from within.

- Learn from others – watch and ask.

- Teach yourself through honest evaluation.
  Discuss as a team.

- Get a friend to video you.

- Read sailing books and articles.

- Develop a system to record accurately
  anything you learn. Not only will writing it
  down make you think about it, but you
  have a record for the future.

- Set yourself goals for improvement.

Training versus racing

The temptation is to race whenever possible
and not to actually train outside races. This
leads to a reluctance to try anything new.
Practice boathandling both in and out of the
racing situation. Boatspeed work is very often
best practised in a two- or three-boat tuning
session.

CONCLUSION

Not many sports offer the variety of challenges
set by racing a modern high-performance
boat around a new-style course. Initially, it
can seem impossible to get to the front of
the fleet. Don't panic! Rapid progress can be
made by breaking down all the areas of the
sport and addressing them one by one.
Commit to honest analysis and a determination
to learn and improve through reading,
watching, listening, experimenting, goal
setting, and practising.

Sailing high-performance sailboats is good fun
and little can match the satisfaction of racing
your boat around the course faster than
anybody else. We hope you can put into
practice some of our methods contained in this
book and if it helps anybody to enjoy the
immense feeling of satisfaction success in our
sport has given us, then it will have achieved
its goal. Good luck and good sailing!

Recommended reading

Helming to Win
Ian Pinnell & Lawrie Smith
In this well illustrated book two former yachtsmen of the Year explain how to steer a boat to win. Covers all wind strengths, all sea conditions and all points of sailing.

Sailpower
Lawrie Smith & Andrew Preece
This major new title in the Sail to Win series cuts through the technical jargon of sailing theory to give you a grasp of the principles that will make you sail faster.

Wind Strategy (2nd edition)
David Houghton
How to predict the wind over the area of the racecourse. Now revised and expanded to include information on using local data to predict the wind, and examples of wind planning at a number of major regatta venues.

Tactics (2nd edition)
Rodney Pattisson
Out-manoeuvre the rest of the fleet with the new edition of this best-selling handbook. The new edition is updated and expanded by 50% to include Match Racing, Team Racing, Offwind Starts and Racing Near the Shore.

Tuning Your Dinghy
Lawrie Smith
Here is a logical, systematic approach to the problem of setting up your boat and fine-tuning it for maximum speed on all points of sailing. Includes a troubleshooting section.

Race Training
Rick White
These drills will make you a champion. "It is the fastest way to improve your skills", Head Coach, Swiss Olympic Team.

Crewing to Win
Andy Hemmings
The crew of a racing boat is as important as the helmsman. This is the only book to cover every aspect of crewing from club level to planning an Olympic campaign. RYA recommended.

Mental & Physical Fitness for Sailing
Alan Beggs, John Derbyshire & Sir John Whitmore
Once you've tuned your boat, if you want to win races you'll need to tune your mind and body too. An Olympic coach and psychologist explain how.

The Rules in Practice
Bryan Willis
The Racing Rules for dinghy sailors, windsurfers and yachtsmen, applied to real life situations and illustrated with helpful photographs of model boats. Contains parts I, IV and V of the rules.

Sails (2nd edition)
John Heyes
Sails are the driving force behind any boat, so it is important to get them right. This expanded edition now covers yacht and dinghy sails, and includes a useful 'faultfinder' chapter.

Protests & Appeals
Bryan Willis
This is a guide for sailors ad protest committees. Learn how to protest, defend a protest or appeal. Vital after expensive collisions!

Tuning Yachts & Small Keelboats
Lawrie Smith
Lawrie Smith advises on how to adjust the mast and sails for maximum boatspeed. 'An ideal shortcut to an understanding of what makes a yacht tick' – Yachts & Yachting.

Racing Crew (2nd Edition)
Malcolm McKeag & Bill Edgerton
A comprehensive manual from the RYA Keelboat Coach on crewing a small racing yacht. Covers every manoeuvre. Fully illustrated.

For a free full-colour brochure write, phone or fax
Fernhurst Books, Duke's Path, High Street, Arundel, West Sussex.
Tel: 01903 882277. Fax: 01903 882715.